THE
DRIVING
INSTRUCTOR'S
GUIDE TO
EFFECTIVE
SELLING
SKILLS

Dedicated to Stuart, who made it all possible.

Do not fall into the error of the artisan who boasts of twenty years experience in his craft while in fact he has had only one year of experience – twenty times.

The Analects of Confucius

THE
DRIVING
INSTRUCTOR'S
GUIDE TO
EFFECTIVE
SELLING
SKILLS

EDWARD BAKER

KOGAN
PAGE

YOURS TO HAVE AND TO HOLD

BUT NOT TO COPY

First published in 1996

Kogan Page Limited
120 Pentonville Road
London N1 9JN

British Library Cataloguing in Publication Data

A CIP record for this book is available from the British Library

ISBN 0 7494 1899 0

Typeset by Northern Phototypesetting Co Ltd, Bolton
Printed in England by Clays Ltd, St Ives plc

Contents

Contents

1

THE NEED FOR SELLING SKILLS

THE REVOLVING DOOR OF FAILURE

Each and every year, 8000 or so hopeful individuals set out on the long road to becoming an Approved Driving Instructor (ADI). As Nature, in the form of the dreaded Parts Two and Three, takes its course, this number is whittled down to perhaps a quarter of the above. The bad news does not stop there, however. Of those who survive the training process, as many as a third will leave the driving instruction business within their first year with varying degrees of bitterness. Another third will quit by the end of year two. What is going on?

The conventional wisdom quoted by many a sad instructor is that there are just too many teachers and not enough pupils. Or again, some schools charge such ridiculously low rates that effective competition is impossible. Those who feel this way will say that they were cheated, that no one ever warned them of the grim statistics. Their excuses for failure sound very plausible until it is realised that they are just that — excuses. Within five miles of any instructor complaining about lack of work you will find another with too much work. Each has passed Part Three, each occupies the same economic niche, each faces the same running costs and yet one is prospering and one is starving.

If you investigate any selling situation (and make no mistake, that is what this is), you will find the above holds true. Whether the product is financial services or double glazing, fitted kitchens or satellite television, you will hear the same complaints about price and competition. And they are not true there either! Such complaints are nearly always a smokescreen to cover an underlying problem with the individual salesperson concerned. That is a bitter pill to swallow but, in order to move from failure to success, swallowed it must be.

JUST HOW DO YOU EARN YOUR LIVING?

At this point, the average ADI will be asking what has all this to do with me? The answer is everything. Most ADIs have a totally wrong idea as to how they earn their living. The problem begins just after qualification when the joy at having succeeded where so many have failed turns into something else. Ask any ADI how he or she makes money. The usual response, together with a bemused grin, is something like, 'I earn a living by teaching people to drive, I'm a teacher'.

That simply is not so. You or any other ADI earn your living by *selling* your skills as a teacher, and there is a world of difference between the two things. This may sound like splitting hairs but it is the biggest mental hurdle you will have to leap if you want to make money. Compare the situation of an ADI with, say, a mathematics teacher in a school. If all the mathematics teacher's pupils decide to skip class because the teacher is arrogant, charmless or unexciting it does not make any difference to the teacher's salary: that will go into the bank at the end of the month, regardless. Questions may be asked but the money will still arrive even during an investigation. Moreover, the pupils will be brought back by a mixture of threats and compulsion.

Now contrast this situation with your own lot as an ADI. Whether you are a franchisee or an independent, you will only make money if you have pupils to teach. If pupils do not appear or decide that they do not like you, you are in trouble. Nobody is going to force them to come back to you either!

Your success (or lack of it) as an ADI depends on your ability as a salesperson. Technical skills are neither here nor there — you can have a grading higher than the inflation rate of a banana republic and still not make money. If you cannot sell your services you are in deep, deep trouble. The Driving Standards Agency (DSA) will not take you off the road for this gap in your training; cash-flow, depression and debt will take care of that.

Before you can teach, you must first sell, a fact overlooked by the entire ADI training process. You must learn to convert all the prospects who get in your car into paying pupils. You are, and must be, a salesperson before you can be an instructor.

WHAT MAKES A SALESPERSON?

By this point, you should be convinced that you are indeed a sales-person. The look of horror that spreads across an ADI's face when confronting this issue usually stems from what he or she imagines a salesperson to be.

A salesperson, to those who have met bad examples, is someone who pesters and bullies. Someone who twists arms and makes people do things they do not want to. Someone who is shifty and full of tricks. No wonder 'sale' is a four-letter word!

A salesperson, a good salesperson, is something very different to the above. A salesperson is someone who makes dreams and aspirations come true. Someone who helps you to understand the good points and bad points of a decision and shows you alternatives. Someone who leaves you feeling good and satisfied.

Whether you are a good salesperson or a bad one is entirely down to you. The market that you are in is not difficult; indeed, most salespeople would give their eye-teeth to be in such a situation. Not only is your product desirable to both young and old alike, it is a legal requirement. Ask any double glazing or insurance person how they would feel about that. When they have stopped laughing they will ask you why you are not cleaning up!

You do not need to be a bully or a 'hard-sell' merchant. What you do need to be, however, is a good salesperson. Sell solutions to problems, sell freedom, sell dreams. Sell the goal, not lessons.

THE SALES PERSONALITY

Once an ADI has accepted reluctantly the need to be a salesperson, one last obstacle is generally thrown up, ie, you need to be born with a sales personality, that you have either got it or you have not. It is amazing how people accept this line; after all, were you born an ADI or teaching personality?

The word 'personality' originally comes from a Latin word meaning 'mask' as used in their plays. It was an outward expression of inner content, a sort of shorthand for character. 'Personality' is a tool and you need to examine your own in this light with a sense of detachment.

Everyone has different personalities depending on the situation in which they find themselves. Sometimes they overlap but in general they are separate; we have roles as spouse, employee, friend etc and behave accordingly. By now you will have already established an ADI personality. You might be flippant and funny, serious and scientific, firm or supportive, that is your choice. What must not happen, however, is that you try to sell in teaching mode. You will need to have different attitudes, ask different questions, watch for different signs. This is not insincerity, it is about responses and reflexes.

The sales personality can be developed through study and practice. It is no different from the process you went through for Part Three. Get it right and you will make yourself very busy and very successful.

THE REAL COMPETITION

Coming to terms with your role as a salesperson will help you to face up to the real 'competititon' — yourself.

Much negative rubbish is talked about the shortage of pupils in the UK. This is rubbish for several reasons. Aside from the self-renewing client base of 17-year-olds, new attitudes and regulations are extending the life of pupils both before and after a test. There are new arrivals to the country who need conversion courses; there are people coming off bans; there are people needing refresher courses and much, much more. In short, there is a lot of work to be had.

There is an element of truth in the competition myth, however.

There are many ADIs who are earning less than their potential because they cling to obsolete practices and attitudes. Their only response to a shortage of hours is to cut prices which, in turn, prompts someone else to drop. The result is a spiral of decline for everyone who participates in this useless exercise.

Your main competition is your lack of interest or faith in your selling skills. Offer a high quality service and be proud of the price you charge. Develop yourself fully and you will not even notice that other ADIs exist.

ABOUT THIS BOOK

The purpose of this book is to help you realise your full earning potential as an ADI. The techniques you will encounter here have all been field-tested and they all work. Whether or not they do for you is down to you. If you so wish you can cling to your self-justifying excuses and continue to live through famine and feast. On the other hand, you can decide to change how you operate and enjoy what you do and make money from it.

There is an oft-quoted story in sales circles. Two boys try to trick an old man sitting in a park. One of the boys says, 'Let's fool the old man. I'll catch a bird and hide it inside my hands and you ask him if it's alive or dead. If he says it's dead I'll open my hands and let it fly away. If he says it's alive I'll give it a squeeze and crush it.' So, the boys caught the bird and went to ask the old man the question. He pondered for a moment and then said, 'The answer is in your hands.'

The answer is in your hands.

2
PLANNING FOR SUCCESS

THE PLANNING PROCESS

'If you plan to go nowhere, that's where you'll end up' is one of the most quoted expressions to be heard in sales circles. It is also one of the most accurate. Like its sister saying — 'Failure to plan is planning to fail' — it encapsulates a principle on which you will stand or fall. That principle is control, and this in turn springs from having a clear business plan. All businesses need a plan to function at their best and this applies as much to a one-person driving school as to a multinational company. A good business plan is the route map that will get you to where you want to be and will, if necessary, pull you back from the edge of disaster.

THE PRAMKU FORMULA

To help you plan effectively, make use of the PRAMKU formula. This means that your goals must be:

- Precise.
- Realistic.
- Achievable.
- Meaningful.
- Known.
- Understood.

Precise in this context means that you have very specific objectives in mind. 'Earning more money' or 'Having more pupils' are not precise targets; 'Earning £20,000 pa' or 'Seeing five new prospects a week' are.

Realistic means just that. Do not set yourself goals that are impossible to achieve from your present occupation. Silly figures belong in daydreams, not plans.

Achievable ties in with the above. A figure may be realistic, but is it achievable by you right now? Can you make your targets without burning yourself out or wrecking relationships?

Meaningful goals will give you spirit. There is no point setting yourself a money-driven programme when what you really want is three holidays abroad a year and no night work. Your plans are your own, not anyone else's.

Known goals are goals shared with a spouse, partner or any other significant person in your life. They need to know what you want to support you.

Understood means that you realise the work rates, performance targets and hours that will deliver your targets.

INTRODUCING THE YEAR PLANNER

In Appendix 1 (p. 113) you will find the single most effective tool in making your dreams come true, other than sweat! This is the year planner and, as its name suggests, it is to be used at the beginning of each calendar year. If you find yourself starting out mid-year though, do not worry — make a short-term version and catch up at the year end.

To get the most out of your year planner take an enlarged photocopy of it and hide yourself away from the world (see hotel days, Chapter 7, p. 88). This will take most of a day, but it will soon repay the time you spend with money!

The year planner is self-explanatory and contains its own prompts; the following notes might be useful, however, as you work through each section.

Personal Objectives

It all starts here! What do you really want from the year ahead in human terms? Is there anything in your life style which you feel is missing or something of which you would rather be rid? In this section you should list whatever you feel is important, from losing weight (how much?) to buying a new house (also how much — remember the PRAMKU formula).

Work-related Objectives

This section not only relates to income, but also to items like hours to be worked, holidays to be taken and so on. If you want a new car or a different client group, put this down too.

Self-assessment

Do you have any faults or deficiencies as a salesperson or as an instructor? Identify them in as cool and critical a fashion as you can.

Outgoings

You need to determine these as exactly as you can. Itemise every foreseeable cost, no matter how trivial. Once you have the total you can then calculate how much you need to earn each week and each month.

Calendar

Before you start to number crunch decide how many weeks you intend to work in the coming year. Put down on paper your main holidays, any days off per week, and then add on down-time for illness or problems with the car. Deduct the figure you have arrived at from the year and see what is left. This then requires a simple calculation to set your work rate ie, target figure ÷ working weeks.

Achieving Target Figures

In this section you will break down the working week into its components to give you even tighter control. Some of the practices listed may be unfamiliar, but you will find them explained in detail in other parts of this book.

Action Plan

Gather together the ambitions you have identified along with your income figures. Commit to paper how you intend to deliver each one.

Contract

You are now going to sign a contract with yourself. This will explain your holiday entitlement, your terms of service and your income. It may sound silly but it contains an important psychological principle.

THE WORKING WEEK

After determining how many weeks you want to work in the year, the next thing to do is to put some structure into them. Begin with an empty week planner (Appendix 1, p. 121) and carry out the same routine as before but on a smaller scale. First, put a line through the days when you are *not* available (hobbies, family time, rest days etc). Refuse to be an externally controlled workaholic — it is not desirable and it is not necessary.

You can then move on to each day itself and decide what hours you work between. This may sound like heresy — an ADI goes out whenever — but if you use the sales techniques to be found throughout this book you can work sensible hours and still make money.

The time left during your working week will probably need to accommodate the following activities.

Trial Lessons/First Meetings

Whatever you choose to call your first encounter with a new prospect, it is one of the most vital components of any week. Because such meetings are usually discounted or free, there is a great temptation to put them off in favour of lessons. This is comparable to letting your tank run dry before thinking about petrol and is the cause of most boom-and-bust cycles. You need to see between two and five new prospects each week. The ideal is one a day; this may sound implausible but if you use the methods described later it is quite easy.

Lessons

Lessons are important too, of course! Not all lessons are equal, however. Some are a criminal waste of time and energy. These are the single, one-hour lessons booked from week to week. Even when working in a tight radius of your home, such lessons increase the length of your day without increasing its productivity. In fact productivity goes down because of the mileage and time wasted moving between pupil and pupil. Remember, you only earn when someone else is driving!

The best way to overcome the problems associated with one-hour lessons is to avoid doing them altogether. Make two hours your minimum tuition period and stick to it except for very special cases. For this approach to succeed you will need to sell the benefit of doing two-hour lessons to your pupil. As always in this sort of situation, you should encourage the prospect to do what you want by demonstrating the advantages:

> Mick, one two-hour session will do more for your confidence and co-ordination than four one-hour lessons. Look at the money you will save!

or again:

> Janice, the reason why two-hour sessions are effective is this: if you go to the gym you'll probably spend 30 or so minutes warming up before you can do the real business. It's the same with driving. In a one-hour lesson you're out of the car just when it's beginning to do you the most good.

There are myriad other reasons you can give for your preference (driving somewhere different, new routes etc). More details on selling two-hour lessons are to be found in Chapter 8 (p. 105) and Appendix 2 (pp. 134–5).

You could, of course, always try to buy the sale by offering a deal on a double slot but this borders on another topic, that of lesson pricing itself.

The hourly rate that you set is not as big a factor in choosing an instructor as unsuccessful ADIs try to make out. At the end of the day people are buying *you* and what you represent. If people like you, they will buy; if they do not, they will not, it is as simple as that. If price was the real key issue then those charging the least would be busy and the more expensive schools quiet. In reality the situation is almost the opposite of this and there is a good reason — sales skills.

Setting a rate can be accomplished through laborious calculations or, more simply, by checking out what the price of the nearest big school is and going just slightly under. Be proud of your price and don't crumble when challenged about it. You will find methods of dealing with price shoppers in the next chapter.

There is one golden rule in price setting and that is *never reduce price in order to attract pupils*. Don't try to buy your way out of what is a selling situation by devaluing your hard-won ability. All it will do is make you angry, cynical and useless, and there is always someone who will undercut you! People will pay a top rate for what they believe to be a top-notch service. Make sure that you provide one and charge accordingly.

Tests

Tests need not be the nightmare that many ADIs turn them into. Again, there is a simple rule — *never let a pupil book their own test*. If you relinquish responsibility for this you also relinquish control. It is pre-ordained by fate that if you let the pupil take charge he or she will pick a date that you cannot possibly manage. Not even a driving school code number (and you thought that was clever!) will make you physically able to fit in the hours that are required by random bookings close to existing work.

Controlling tests will be discussed fully in a later chapter. For now it is sufficient to say that you must act like a mountaineer sending provisions ahead to the next camp.

Mock Tests

Mock tests generally are used as a part of tuition but they can be money earners in their own right. Combine these with test observations and you can do wonders (Chapter 7).

Theory Tuition/Passplus

Recent changes in legislation have increased drastically the shelf-lives of learner drivers both pre- and post-test. The implications of these changes are considerable in terms of your earning potential. Theory tuition, in particular, can help you make more money while at the same time reducing your working hours. The companion volume to this book, *The Driving Instructor's Guide to Teaching the Theory L Test* (Baker, forthcoming 1996), will help you cash in on this crucial area.

Passplus, as of writing, has made little impact. The idea is excellent and the product saleable, but the problem again lies in low-level sales skills. The key is to think in terms of multiple sales to pupils, not just one-shot driving lessons.

Administration

Each working week also will involve some time for administration. Most ADIs regard this as a necessary evil. However, Chapter 6 will make it earn money for you, which lends a certain allure.

ACTIONS INTO NUMBERS

With the key elements of a typical week identified you can begin the process of filling in the relevant section of your year planner. Determine the mix and match of your products and allocate target figures to each of them, ie, how many lessons are you planning on, how many assesssments etc.

In setting your figures do not forget peripheral sales. This again comes down to thinking about multiple sales instead of just 'straight' driving lessons. You can, for instance, hire out videos you have purchased or made. This works on the following lines: after explaining the value of supplementary learning you loan the video at the cost of, say, £15. On its safe return a few days later you return £10 and keep £5. Insignificant on its own, yes, but if carried out with 20 pupils a week and added into your overall prof-its …

A second bolt-on sale applies to those who have just passed their test with you. Their next problem is insurance. Of course, you have the answer. Following the recommendations in Chapter 3 you will have set in place a relationship with a broker. You pass the pupil's name on (with his or her permission) to your contact. If the sale is made you get 50 per cent of the commission — it is that simple. No forms, no effort, no sweat. You just have to remember to do it. One of these a week should be enough over the course of a year to pay for those holidays you want!

Finally, you can sell memberships to car recovery schemes or anti-theft devices. Again, keep things uncomplicated — you want extra cash, not headaches.

NUMBERS INTO ACTION

The completed year planner is one of the keys to profitable tuition. The other is effective time management. You will find repeated at several points in this book the maxim: 'If you don't control your diary, it will control you'. Far too many ADIs let themselves be pushed around by events instead of controlling them. By now though, you should have an inkling of how total control can be achieved. As your own 'employer' it is up to you whether you are a cheap hired hand or a valued member of staff with good terms and conditions.

The essence of diary control is planning. Your days can be as structured as those of any employed person, you just need to stop behaving like a dog jumping through hoops. When a pupil demands impossible times or deals, refuse. When you seem to be so busy with existing pupils that you have not got time for new ones, find it.

A useful aid to diary control is a 'things to do' sheet (Appendix 1). Complete one of these at the end of each day and work through it. Don't try to remember things, write them down.

You can, if you wish, take diary control and time planning to very sophisticated lengths. Using different coloured pens you can record just how your time is spent and what it is worth. To be honest, however, you need not go that deep. Just control your pupils' training with the methods discussed later and ensure that you see one new prospect a day.

One last comment on time. Don't waste the time spent travelling between pupils in dwelling on morbid newscasts or miserable thoughts. Buy some pre-prepared motivational tapes on sales technique, or put together your own music tape. Choose tunes that make you feel dynamic, powerful or exciting so that you arrive at your next pupil or prospect feeling like the world is yours for the taking.

PROFIT CIRCLES

A seemingly self-evident but often overlooked point is that you only make money when someone else is behind the wheel. Time spent moving between pupils needs to be kept to a bare minimum. The real crunch involves your teaching methods (see below) but a concept that can help you is that of profit circles.

Profit circles make for both richer and shorter days. Take a map of your area and, using a compass and marker, encircle the roads within a few miles of your home or office. Label this circle A and then repeat the process over wider circles till you reach the point where it is no longer feasible to offer tuition.

Circle A represents the optimum place to do business. The size of the area will vary somewhat according to population density but wherever you are the distances need to be kept very short. You need to ask yourself the following questions about the patch:

- What ex-pupils can I contact for recommendations?
- What centres of influence (colleges, firms etc) can I contact?
- What training routes can I use to avoid congestion and delay?
- Which garages offer the best deals on fuel?
- Which shops can I advertise in for little or no cost?
- Is there a church hall or school I can use for theory training nights?

Armed with the above information you can put your strategy into effect (see also Chapter 3).

Circle B is not quite as good as circle A but it is still productive. Use the pupil control methods shown in later chapters to create dedicated days. In addition, try and up your minimum lesson to three hours.

Circle C is the outer limits! If you have to operate in this area out of dire necessity, make prepayment in full conditional.

In the beginning your circles will be very wide. With practice and diligence, however, you will see them shrink until the bulk of your work is on your doorstep.

TRADITIONAL VERSUS MODERN METHODS

Traditionally, driving skills have always been taught on the basis of a few hours each week done over an indefinite period. The pupil's abilities are sharpened until at last he or she is submitted for testing, with this event to follow some time later.

More and more students, however, are electing to go on 'crash' or intensive courses. In this method a needs-based analysis is carried out and tuition worked backwards from a chosen test date.

This is not the place to study the merits and demerits of each system from a technical point of view. In sales terms though, there is much that bears thinking about.

The tables comparing the two systems offer serious food for thought. Most of the disadvantages of the intensive system turn out to be advantages when considered from another point of view ie, higher level of pupil commitment, the need for prosperous clients and so forth. In fact the only thing that can be said against

Advantages and disadvantages of the intensive system

Advantage	Disadvantages
■ Different, new, removes price conscious clients ■ Calls for a higher level of commitment ■ Yields predictable, stable income ■ Makes for shorter daytime hours ■ Reduces mileage ■ Reduces unpaid time ■ Fewer pupils required per week and year ■ Reduces stress caused by unpredictable hours and rushing between lessons	■ Harder to sell

Note: This comparison is made on sales/economic terms only

Advantages and disadvantages of the traditional system

Advantages	Disadvantages
■ Easy to sell ■ Commonly known and understood ■ Allows for pupils not wanting to spend much money ■ Low level commitment asked for	■ Easy to undercut ■ Old fashioned, lacks glamour ■ Encourages pupils not wanting to spend much money ■ Frequently cancelled because of lack of commitment ■ More pupils required per week thus increasing travel time and costs ■ Subject to seasonal factors eg Christmas ■ Pupils easily poached by other ADIs ■ Produces unstable income due to wild fluctuations ■ Leads to boredom and dissatisfaction

Note: 1. This comparison is made on sales/economic terms only
2. It can be noticed that most of the 'advantages' can also be perceived as disadvantages

intensive courses is their higher, one-off cost, and this is a selling problem rather than a serious objection.

It is usual to ask for payment in full before the start of a concentrated course and this removes the problem of cancelled hours in one fell swoop. Fewer pupils per week means lower mileage and more time teaching. Additionally, the sort of pupil who will do a course is more than likely to take a week off work in which to do it! Courses have a lot going for them.

The intensive course is the wave of the future whatever its rights and wrongs. A fixed price and duration make it very attractive to today's more sophisticated learner driver. Nobody is suggesting that you abolish odd hours altogether, but think what one prepaid course a week could do for your business and lifestyle. You will find out how to sell them in Chapter 5.

CANCELLATIONS

The main bugbear of any ADI's existence is the pupil who fails to show up or who cancels at very short notice. By the time that the pupil informs you that the budgie is gravely ill or that little Damion needs a fang pulling out, it is certain that it will be too late for you to put anything productive in place of the lesson. The theory is, of course, that the ADI charges all the same, but in practice it never seems to work out this way. An ADI will not want to upset a good pupil by making an issue of it; a bad pupil will not pay anyhow. The net result is that you lose money. If this happened only occasionally it would be bearable if somewhat annoying but it happens every week. Over the year that means a lot of cash lost.

There are a number of measures that you can take to protect yourself from the effects of cancellations. The first step is to put prepaid courses at the top of your agenda. The second is to charge for one lesson in advance, sweetening the pill by telling the pupil how it will help him or her:

> *ADI:* I'm glad you've enjoyed this first lesson. One reason I can afford to spend more time with my pupils is that I never have any cancellations to worry about. Because I know exactly what I'm doing, I don't have to rush off trying to fill up gaps and I can take a bit longer, like we just have done on gears. I think that's important, don't you?
>
> *Prospect:* I think it's great! Usually I get less than an hour, not more!
>
> *ADI:* That's right! My students help me to help them though. What I do is hold a retainer which is the cost of one double lesson. I don't have to mess around changing things then, so nobody suffers. If you need to miss, don't worry, it's taken care of. Of course, if you don't miss any training, as I hope you won't, you'll get it back. You get a cash bonus for passing — is that fair enough?

With this measure in place you can treat cancellations with impunity — they become paid rest time! If a pupil does miss, start the process over again. You need to make this mandatory. If a prospect will not play ball then he or she should be ditched. Look after the good ones and get rid of the bad.

Incidentally, by using this mechanism you have also created a self-renewing contingency fund. At any given time you will be holding the lesson value of 20 or 30 pupils, and this should help you out with cash-flow problems or holidays.*

CONCLUSION

Along with sales skills, the only thing that separates a prospering ADI from one who is starving is the ability to plan and control. With practice you should be able to book your work several months in advance, if not longer. (Sell courses for half-term,

---

* A pupil who does not miss training is, of course, due some money back. If you suggest a day or so before the test that they might want to use this bonus on extra tuition however …

summer holidays, Christmas — create your own assembly line.) If you get this bit right you will take the sting out of self-employment and you can enjoy its benefits.

Now all you need are some prospects.

3
PROSPECTS

THE NUMBERS GAME

Selling is a numbers game. See enough people on a regular basis and no matter how tongue-tied, inept or shy you are you will make a sale. The biggest difference between an instructor who is making money and one who is not usually involves the number of new prospects they see each week.

The successful instructor always sees his or her target number of prospects each week no matter what else has to be altered (the sole exceptions are tests). Existing clients, if you have bonded with them properly, can always be asked for a favour. A new prospect, on the other hand, has nothing to judge you by except your response to his or her problem.

Break the chain of seeing new people and you are heading for feast and famine, overwork and enforced idleness. Remember that for every pupil who passes the test you will need at least two prospects as potential replacements. But how do you find replacements? Just how do you fill the tank?

PUMP UP THE VOLUME

The 'pumps' from which you can draw off new prospects — that is, people who have not bought from you *yet* — can be summarised as follows:

1. Printed literature (newspapers, magazines etc).
2. Peripherals (cards, pens etc).
3. Presentations (talks, swap meets etc).
4. Telephone calls.
5. Referrals.

Of these, only the first four will be discussed in this Chapter. The last source, referrals, is so powerful a tool that it merits a section of its own. In fact, if you really master the technique of referrals it is unlikely that you will need any further advertising. Until you reach that point though you will need to cast your lines deep and wide.

GETTING INTO PRINT: NEWSPAPERS AND THE LIKE

Perhaps the most obvious place to advertise your service is in the local newspapers. They are cheap, consulted on a daily basis and reach a massive audience — or at least that is what the sales representative on the other end of the phone will tell you! The reality of the situation can be very different. It is possible to spend a small fortune in this way and achieve only mediocre results.

When dealing with newspapers the most important thing to remember is not to get sold to yourself. On no account should you allow newspaper advertisements to swallow up your entire advertising budget. Scepticism, caution and diversity are the watchwords here.

Select your newspaper with care. A daily with a big circulation over a wide area may sound promising but if it brings in calls from outside your profit circles (Chapter 2) what is the point? Again, a daily is just what it says, a cheap something to be disposed of every 24 hours. A weekly freepress might have more staying power. Only local research will show you what you need. Ask around friends and neighbours before parting with cash.

Once you have decided on the paper for the job you need to think about method and message. Say 'no' to lavish spreads and panels that will do the media barons more good than you.

The most cost-effective way to advertise is in those back page lines which people who want something scan with microscopic intensity. You might think that setting up in the 'driving' section is a waste of cash because it is there that all your competitors will be peddling their wares. All to the good; a quick glance through will show you that most of the advertisers have had a charisma bypass operation. Their lines are so dull and predictable that they really are a waste of money.

The TEA Formula

Advertisements in this sort of section need to be punchy and well focused — you have got maybe a dozen words before the exercise becomes a costly turn off. You need to be fresh. You need to be different. You need to remember the TEA formula:

- Tantalise.
- Excite.
- Assure.

The short, snappy message you have got to deliver should provide just enough information to arouse curiosity; it should excite by offering a solution to a defined problem; it should assure by establishing financial goalposts.

Here is how the formula could work in practice. Supposing, after your planning stage, you have decided that multiple test failures offer a low mileage, high income source of revenue. Your line could read something like this:

KEEP FAILING? INTENSIVE PROBLEM-SOLVING
MODULES FROM £148, TEST INC! PHONE 1234567.

Study these words for a moment. Both the problem and the remedy are stated clearly. That remedy is a bit exciting and mysterious. (I have had lots of lessons and they did not work, but a module ...?) The *from* figure assures the reader that it will not be a wallet extraction procedure; and the *test inc* sounds like a freeby.

This can be varied to suit a number of situations, for example:

> OVERSEAS DRIVERS! NEEDS ANALYSIS AND
> REPORT FOR ONLY £10.00. RING 7891011!

or again:

> DRIVE BY CHRISTMAS! BOOK YOUR COURSE NOW,
> ONLY £399, TEST INCLUDED! RING 7654321 NOW!

Spend a little time reviewing the benefits you identified in the previous Chapter and work them into easily swallowed capsules. Develop four of these so that you can use them in rotation to catch the eye from week to week.

A word of warning. Check for your advertisement each week. Most papers pay their telesales personnel low wages and the result is a high turnover in staff. Whoever takes over your account may be more interested in new business than yours. You can never get back a lost week even if they give you a free one.

Business Directories

Yellow Pages, Thomson's Directories etc are great places to be seen in, but be careful how you go about it. Timing is vital. If you cannot get in before the deadlines don't bother. Don't commit a huge chunk of your budget to something that will not yield results for months.

Bad Press?

You can end up advertising in everything from *The Times* to the 'Rabbit Fanciers Monthly' if you are not careful. It is easy to say yes, especially when a good telesales offers persuasive arguments in favour. Everyone from local charity magazines to multinational-owned papers will be after you, so watch out!

PERIPHERALS

Peripherals offer an interesting alternative to the media, but once again you need to be careful. You can put your name on almost

anything, but leave the pens and other gimmicks to the big schools
— they can afford them! Instead try some of the not so glamorous
methods listed below and prepare to be amazed.

A Short Essay On The Business Card

All too often, the humble business card is dismissed as a mere
afterthought. Used properly, however, it is a tool that can bring in
prospects by the dozen.

First, catch your business card! The same principles mentioned
earlier apply to content and layout. These days cards can be made
on a DIY basis on machines available in stations or motorway service areas but it is cheaper to get them produced professionally on
the scale you will need them. This sounds like another cost but it
can actually be achieved for nothing.

A card has two sides. Use the front for yourself but make the
back available to an advertiser who has an interest in your client
group — insurance brokers, car dealers or garages for instance. To
such businesses your proposition makes good economic sense;
you will be handing out cards to a target audience and they will
benefit from your tacit recommendation. The literal flip-side to
this, of course, is that they can hand out cards too. Approach several businesses to build up a huge stock. Start with your own
insurance broker — he is not going to turn you down, is he? Keep
trying; whatever the result, it is good sales experience.

Now that you have cards by the thousand, what to do with
them? You can give them out to everyone you meet, of course, but
that is only half the story. Whenever you pay a bill use a card
instead of a compliments slip or letter. As it lands on a desk it
might just catch someone's eye and bring you a new client.

Another way to move cards is to leave piles of them in shops or
businesses friendly to your cause (see below, Centres of
Influence).

A slight variation on this is to ask every regular client to pin one
of your cards to his or her workplace notice-board. This has the
added advantage that an enquirer will be able to get a firsthand
report.

The best way to move cards is to give them a nominal value as part of an introductory offer (half-price lesson or trial to the bearer). Get your existing clients to customise cards with personal messages and tell them to pass them on to friends and relatives. In turn, you will make both feel important by offering a free or reduced session. There is no such thing as free, however. The discount you offer should be rolled up in the all-inclusive price that you are going to quote!

Shop Window Advertising

Shop window advertising — either with the ubiquitous business card or a specially prepared item — offers a lot to the hungry instructor. First, it really can be done on a shoestring. Second, the effect is instantaneous and measurable. Third, it allows you to concentrate your work in a particular neighbourhood or street. The passing of your car will add to its effect and will help make for low mileage, high profit tuition.

As with the newspaper lines, design cards that appeal to different markets. Cards offering courses at say Christmas or half-term are very effective. If you keep a card in a window on a regular basis then check it every so often for colour (they fade in the sun and need renewing).

Car Stickers/Headboards

Covering your car with stickers will make it work for you even when it is not moving. A powerful one-liner is best — use the TEA formula again. When people scribble down the number on the palm of their hand or on a piece of paper you have a very excited prospect.

PRESENTATIONS AND ACTIVE PROSPECTING

It is a common but mistaken belief that the only way to obtain clients is to advertise and then to sit back and wait. There are, in fact, a variety of excellent techniques whereby you can actually go out and bring them in. Active prospecting puts you in charge of the numbers game. Even better, usually it does not cost anything.

One Of Yours, One Of Mine: Swap Meets

A painless way to begin active prospecting is to get into or organise a swap meet. This is an American concept in which you get together over breakfast or lunch with people who are in related fields. Each participant has to bring a couple of names along who can be contacted by one of the others. For instance, as an instructor you might offer the names of newly-qualified pupils. These could be of interest to a broker, car dealership, alarm firm and so on. In turn, they might offer the names of people needing tuition.

Arrange to meet at a regular time and place but remember that this is business, not pleasure. If people appear who do not keep their side of the deal then exclude them in the future. Once you have the names follow the procedures described in Telephone Skills below.

Centres of Influence

Centres of influence are people or places willing and able to recommend your services. A large firm, for instance, might provide you with leads when they take staff on; a youth association might let you know when one of its members can – legally — drive; and so on.

A great many of your centres of influence will spring from satisfied clients. The law of averages dictates that you will train your share of company directors, club members etc, so take advantage of the fact. You might wish to develop a special deal for the centre, but avoid the idea of a kickback for leads unless the client brings it up. Not only will this cost money, it also gives the thing a certain tackiness. Develop a code of honour, too. It goes without saying that anybody passed on to you gets VIP treatment.

Neighbours, friends, etc can act also as centres of influence. You probably think that everyone in your social orbit knows you are an ADI. You are probably wrong. As you start talking you will be amazed at how many I-wish-I'd-known-thats you will get.

Set yourself a project. Compile a list of 100 people known to you – the neighbours, the postman, where you get your shopping, absolutely anyone. Identify wherever possible how they might be of use — hobbies, contacts, workplace etc.

With the list complete, make a point of talking to each one by a specified date. The aim is not to try and make them pupils but to act as agents for you. The simplest way to do this is to smile and ask them what they are doing these days. They will talk about their job and life — as surely as day follows night, they will then ask about you with the same degree of interest you have shown in them. At this stage highlight your unique selling points. You might even want to give them a few free assessment cards.

Group Talks

As selling is a numbers game, it makes sense to talk to prospects in groups rather than one at a time. If you talk to a single person you have only got one opportunity to sell; talk to 10 or 20 people and the odds are much better. Group talks will localise your business and improve both its quantity and quality. Be warned, however, that the cost in courage and ego is as high as the rewards are great.

Unless you come from a background where you have had experience in group presentations you will probably need some training. There are lots of options from Dale Carnegie at one end of the market to inexpensive adult education courses at the other. Drama groups, debating societies, Chambers of Commerce, all of these and more will give you help in handling audiences (see also Appendix 4).

A good script will then be required to show off your new found skills. This is excellent bad weather work as, indeed, are talks themselves. Isolate the qualities and methods that make you different and build them firmly in. Put it together, take it apart and reassemble until you have got a ten-minute show. Rehearse this on your own, then on video and then in front of friends.

Use a wide variety of props and aids to make you feel safer and the audience more thoughtful. These could be recommended books to pass around, lesson plans or overlays, videos etc. For bigger shows you might want to consider hiring an overhead projector. The impact of visual presentations together with a strong script can work wonders.

With all this done, take the show on the road. Start off on a low level. Ask a passed pupil if they would host a coffee morning or evening, inviting along any friends or neighbours with driving problems. After a short talk and a question-and-answer session make them an offer they cannot refuse — a reduced rate for back-to-back lessons on the same street on the same day. Explain how localising work helps you bring down costs so that they feel it is a bargain rather than a sale. Then proceed as normal.

With a few such sessions under your belt you should be ready for the big time. Expect it to be terrifying, because it will be. Contact groups, colleges, whatever. Don't pay for premises or slots — get invitations. Try to make at least one presentation of either sort a month. In no time at all you will have built up a very healthy client bank.

To quote Winston Churchill in a very different context, this is the end of the beginning. Active prospecting will put you in the driving seat in every sense of the expression.

TELEPHONE SKILLS

So, all of a sudden the advertising has come alive and the phone is ringing like Quasimodo on Acid. All you have to do is pick up the phone and rake in the business, right? Wrong!

The only people who think that selling over the phone is easy are those people who have never had to do it for a living. From the very time the receiver is lifted to the time it is put down, the conversation can go wrong at any moment. Turning initial enquiries into hard bookings is one of the most vital moments in the sales cycle. Unless you take the trouble to get this bit right you might as well not bother advertising.

Who is Talking?

Before discussing the techniques that will bring you success on the telephone it is necessary to decide *who* actually will be at the other end of it. For those working for a school this will be taken care of, but the independent ADI has a number of choices:

1. An answerphone can be used to log return calls to be made after tuition.
2. A partner or spouse can be asked to act as a salesperson/secretary.
3. A paid telesales can be retained.

All of the above options have their merits and demerits. For instance, answering machines are cheap and need little attention. On the other hand a great many people hate talking to them and will just hang up. Then again, the moment of desire and excitement is lost. Most seriously, a taped message allows the competiton to beat you to the punch. If the next number the prospect rings offers a warm, understanding voice you can almost certainly say goodbye to a potential client.

Most ADIs take the route of asking their already long-suffering partners to take the strain. This might be fun at first but as you are hoping for the phone to get red hot it will soon become a nightmare. Quality control tends to suffer also as you have to preface your criticism with a thank you. If the kids are bawling, the dog is barking and the budgie is moulting then you have lost any degree of credibility. If your partner is to act in this capacity you need to have a separate business line and get him or her trained (Appendices 3 and 4).

By far and away the best option is to retain the services of a telesales. Although this will entail a cost it will not be as much as you think and it will increase your business tenfold. Incidentally, a telesales is cheaper and easier to replace than a put-upon or wounded spouse.

A telesales can be recruited from a Job Centre or newspaper. The ideal is someone with experience who wants to work from home on a commission only basis. If this approach is taken your outlay is minimal. All calls are incoming and you only pay out after you yourself have been paid.

In selecting a telesales, look for enthusiasm and warmth, for someone who sounds genuinely interested in people and their driving problems. A sneaky way of checking this is to call them back unexpectedly after an initial talk. The aim is to catch them without their verbal clothes on.

Establish terms and conditions from the outset. Make your commission decent with a bonus for hitting target figures. When it is earned then pay out at once; nothing kills enthusiasm faster than being owed money.

Whoever answers the phone, be it yourself, spouse or telesales, there are rules and attitudes that must be in place. This is about selling, not message taking.

Setting The Sound Stage

A controlled conversation leading to a sale can be as structured and as electifying as a stage play — the only difference is that in this play the audience gets to decide the end! Like a stage play too, this little drama requires props.

Work from a desk or table top if possible. It may sound insultingly obvious but always keep a pen and paper handy (just think about all those times you have been left dangling). A street guide or preferably a map with profit circles is essential. In the early stages of development a mirror is useful. This seemingly useless item is compulsory in many telesales offices and for a good reason. When you smile it sounds in your voice. Try it and see. The mind follows the body just as the body follows the mind. Smiling relaxes you and takes the edge out of your speech.

A tape recorder is very useful too, especially the kind that can be connected to the phone. Tape your voice and study its qualities. Do you sound friendly, confident and enthusiastic? Do you speak or gabble? Take turns with your partner to be salesperson and prospect.

You will need a calculator or an all-inclusive price list for those few clients who force you into offering a figure (see below for how to avoid this). A desk diary is mandatory — if you are running a double diary system (telesales and instructor) — then this must be updated by the ADI the minute a new booking is made.

Two separate forms will be required, masters of which can be found in Appendix 1. The first of these is the bookings form (Client Information Sheet, see p. 126). A good booking form should offer much more than name, address and pick up time. It will provide you with information like how much they have been paying, problems with previous instructors etc, which will help you to help them to say yes.

The second form (New Business Activity Log, see p. 127) is much more painful to use. You need to record how many calls you get each day and where they come from (paper, referral and so on). You also need to record how many of the enquiries you turn into appointments and this is when it can start to hurt. Be brutally honest with these figures — don't make excuses like 'they weren't serious' or 'he's an idiot'. If you attempted a sale then record the fact. Your conversion rate will show you whether you need to alter your style or script. Unless you spot the symptoms you cannot treat the condition.

On the Third Ring …

The phone is ringing but don't be in a hurry to pick it up. An overeager snatch will be a shock to both you and the prospect. Let it ring three times to allow you to clear yourself of negative thoughts and the residue of the last call. Let the prospect settle down and then say 'Good morning' or whatever, like you mean it. Ring a few of your competitors and see how it should not be done!

If you need to, stand up and talk. You may find that this gives you a sense of excitement and authority. Likewise, gesticulate as if the prospect can actually see you; the conviction that you fill yourself with will transmit down the wires. At this stage, as in the first meeting, the prospect is buying *you*. Emotion comes first, logic second. The prospect needs to be relaxed, calmed and praised for making a good decision.

Say What?

You need a script. Writing this will be considerably easier if you have followed the TEA formula. If, for instance, prospects ring about your problem-solving modules or concentrated courses, you have got a convenient launch point. Beware of giving out too many details. Your purpose is to put bums on seats, not to lecture.

Study your benefits list again. If you intend to offer extras like video use or free hours, then spell out your terms and conditions. Any blurring at this point only stores up trouble for the future.

The script that you finally arrive at should not be a bald recitation of facts. In fact, it should not sound like a script at all. You need to build in listening gaps, spaces for objections and questions.

Telephone Exchanges

Excluding personal calls, people are going to call you about only one thing — their driving problems. Because of this it is possible to predict and control the kind of conversation you are going to have. After a little practice you will learn to recognise the prospect type and how to deal with them.

Let us start with a hard, discouraging type, the price shopper. This is the sort of person who will ring around endlessly to find the cheapest deal; he or she is suspicious, arrogant and, because of this attitude, is almost certain to get ripped off. This is how the conversation between a price shopper and someone who has not mastered telephone technique goes:

Salesperson:	Hello, Supersure Driving, how can I help?
Prospect:	Yes, what do you charge an hour?
Salesperson:	Er — £12.
Prospect:	Thanks (click).

Answering a prospect in this fashion helps no one, least of all the prospect. He or she will literally get taken for a ride with someone who promises the moon for nothing. From your position, dealing with a prospect in such a way is going to leave you depressed and exposed to the niggling doubt that you are perhaps charging too much per lesson. Control the conversation. If you are going to lose the booking then at least come out of it feeling morally superior. Here is how a price shopper ought to be handled:

Salesperson:	Hello, Supersure Driving, how can I help?
Prospect:	Yes, what do you charge an hour?
Salesperson:	If you're after the cheapest school in town, sir, I have to say we're not it! If you look through the paper you'll see lots cheaper. What we offer is an excellent pass rate and courses to get you qualified in a week or a month. Cheap we're not. If price is more important than passing, then we might not be the school for you.

At this point, most prospects will tell you that price is not the main issue and you can address their real concerns. Your tone needs to be strong but not aggressive or dismissive. You are saying that you demand respect for hard-earned skills in the form of a just payment. You are reminding the prospect that passing the test is the object, not pseudo-economy. Note the 'we' — even if you are a solo operative you should use this. A 'we' sounds more powerful and also helps to preserve a psychological distance that 'I' does not.

Just occasionally you will get a prospect who will continue to demand a price. Tell them — if they cannot afford it you do not want them anyway. But tell them, do not apologise, then put the phone down before they can!

Questions And Answers

Not all of your enquiries will be like that, so don't worry. Most will be sincerely curious as to what you have got that is different. Nearly all of them are hoping that you are the answer to their prayers. They want to buy and they will buy. Your job is to make it easy for them to say yes.

When a call is in response to your unique service, don't blind the prospect with science. Don't recite and expect them to give in. Use questions and answers to identify their problems and lead them to a decision, ie:

Prospect:	Can you tell me about these problem-solving modules then?
Salesperson:	Certainly madam, is it for yourself?*
Prospect:	No, it's for my boyfriend actually.
Salesperson:	Could I ask a few questions — it'll help me give the right advice. How much driving has he done?
Prospect:	Oh, lots! He's had three tests. I think he gets nervous. He's not much on roundabouts either.
Salesperson:	Let me make a note of that. Roundabouts did you say?

The above exchange has provided you with a supply of material that you can weave into the conversation (nerves, roundabouts etc). More importantly, you are getting the prospect involved. You are treating him or her like a human being instead of reeling off prices. You have respected the prospect's right not to buy.

Pay special attention to the last sentence in this exchange, 'let me make a note of that'. These simple words will lead to more bookings than you would think possible. By obtaining the prospect's tacit permission to write things down you have established the trust required for getting name, address and appointment. You are half-way there. To continue:

* Some texts recommend that you ask for names at this point but it can easily startle the prospect. You can always ask for 'records' later.

Salesperson:	This sounds daft, but why does he want to drive?
Prospect:	He's been promised a job if he can pass his test.
Salesperson:	Great! If he's got strong motivation that's a big help. Is he taking lessons at the moment?
Prospect:	We've just stopped with one school. It was going on and on and doing the same thing every week.
Salesperson:	And how much have you paid for that?
Prospect:	£7 an hour.
Salesperson:	Over how many weeks?
Prospect:	Must be ten months.

The final pieces of the jigsaw are coming in now. What you have is a prospect who is desperate to drive but who is bored stiff with lessons. Price is not the issue. All you need to do is select the tool for the job, in this case a problem-solving module.

Salesperson:	From what you've told me I think your boyfriend's had enough lessons but he's had them too far apart to alter his habits. What we offer are short, tailor-made modules done over a few days. The way we do it he goes in for his test with everything fresh in his mind.
Prospect:	Sounds great. How much?
Salesperson:	That depends on how many modules he needs. We start with a trial lesson at £– – – –, with no commitment or strings attached. At the end of that we'll be able to tell him how much, how long and when. Are mornings or evenings better?

An alternative to the last question is to ask if the prospect is free on, say, a Monday or a Thursday. Don't offer a question that can be answered with a 'no'. Offer alternative yes answers.

The last bit of business is to take names and numbers. Ask the prospect to spell out any unfamiliar road names. With everything settled, read the whole details back to the prospect and say a pleasant goodbye.

Make yourself comfortable with this method of controlling a conversation. Add in jokes or asides to suit your taste but don't leave out sequences and try to go for a booking too soon. Read also the chapter on closes (Chapter 8). These can work on the phone as well as in the car.

The 'Experienced' Driver

Another sort of prospect to whom you will quickly become accustomed is the prospect who has driven for years but not legally. This sort of person generally responds to a brasher, almost conspiratorial attitude. They are like — and often are – naughty little boys who are proud of their daring. Because this sort of prospect is convinced that he can drive already, he usually has an aversion to spending money. He thinks he is getting ripped off. There is no point lecturing this sort of prospect on the error of his ways. You need to stroke his ego and get him into your car. Win his confidence by telling him what it *will not* cost and show you understand his needs. Here is how you can convert this sort of prospect:

Prospect:	Well I've been driving for years, if you know what I mean. Just haven't got round to a test yet.
Salesperson:	I'm with you. What you're telling me is that you can drive, you just need polishing up.
Prospect:	Exactly right pal. How much?
Salesperson:	The thing is, it's harder to give you a price than a complete beginner. If you were a novice we'd be quoting £399 but there's no way you'd need that much, so you can breathe a sigh of relief!
Prospect:	You can say that again!
Salesperson:	The problem is all these years you've been driving you've maybe developed a few habits that might let you down on test.
Prospect:	Bad habits, I know. Like crossing hands.

Salesperson:	That sort of thing. Now how much it costs will depend on how deep those habits are. It shouldn't involve a lot either in money or time. What we need to do is to see you drive. We can give exact figures, and if you want to have your cash ready we can book a test!
Prospect:	When can I go?

My Company is so mean …

Every so often you will get prospects asking for literature. Now you can go to the trouble and cost of having glossy leaflets printed if you really *want* to, but it is important not to see this as opting out of a sales attempt. Go for a booking with firmness and style:

Prospect:	Can you send me some literature then?
Salesperson:	Actually, madam, we don't send literature out because we're so mean.
Prospect:	Oh.
Salesperson:	If we sent out expensive literature, guess who'd end up paying for it? We believe in keeping costs to a minimum so pupils get quality tuition at affordable prices. Of course, most of the information you need is supplied at the first meeting. Is there anything you'd like me to go over again?

Do so, and this time sell a booking! Recognise that the request for literature is in most cases a delaying tactic to avoid making a decision. You have probably used it yourself on other salespeople.

LAST WORDS

Locating new prospects and converting them into bookings is crucial to your success as an ADI. Don't assume it is easy. Read about, develop and practise your phone skills. Treat it like you did your Part Three — it is that important.

4

THE SALES CLIMATE

CREATING THE SALES ENVIRONMENT

Making a decision to purchase, as hopefully you have realised by now, involves much more than price alone. All sorts of factors come into play each and every time we, as human beings, arrive at a positive or negative conclusion. Sometimes we are not even aware of the invisible strings pulling us, but they pull us just the same. Failure to acknowledge this will make your selling unnecessarily difficult.

The place in which you will do the majority of your sales presentation is inside your car. Your car is your office and your stage and you must do everything you can to turn it into an environment conducive to buying by making it appeal to as many senses as possible.

SEEING IS BELIEVING

Sight is the most dominant and powerful of the senses. From the time when our species lacked words and coherent thought, we have always relied on our excellent vision to tell us what is nice and what is nasty. That is as true today as it was a million years ago.

Your prospect will make a decision to buy (or not, as the case may be), within the first 15 seconds of meeting you. Sight will convey the initial parcels of information and it follows, therefore, that you should exploit appearances to the full. The process begins the minute your car drives into view. If your car is shoddy, dirty or cluttered it conveys a lot to your prospect about your attitude to him or her. As the saying goes, you never get a second chance to make a first impression. So make it a good one.

The next thing a prospect sees is you. Hopefully, you will be smiling and warm. A smile can defuse, disarm and comfort some-one who is probably very nervous. Moreover, the act will make you feel better inside. Smiling habitually tends to adjust the inner climate. Some self-help books recommend that you spend a little time each day smiling at the mirror. It is not such a bad idea. If you smile at someone the chances are that they will smile at you and then you will feel happier as well. (Note: if you have ill fitting or discoloured teeth, do something about them.)

Do you dress like one in authority, an instructor about to take responsibility for teaching a life and death skill? Imagine, for a moment, that you decide you do need to visit the dentist after all. As you sit cowering in the reception area a bedraggled, blood and cement spattered wreck walks in and shouts 'Next!' How are you going to feel about that, confident or worried? Likewise, if you went for a bank loan and the manager looked like a pot-smoking layabout, what would that make you do? These are silly examples of course, but there is a serious point involved. We all have expec-tations of what a particular sort of person should be like. The 'uni-form' itself triggers off lots of feelings and associations — think of the sight of a nurse or a priest. The superficial image hits you first and conditions all your responses.

Dress for the first meeting like it was a date or a very important event. Tracksuits and jeans are great after you have turned the prospect into a pupil, but to begin with try and project a strong, responsible image. If necessary, keep some looser clothes in the boot of the car for when you are teaching. (Incidentally, how many ADIs mention dress to their pupils on test?) Leaving aside stupid and sexist comments to female pupils about wearing short skirts, few instructors recognise the fact that examiners are human too. A pupil who looks tidy and respectable might just have an advan-tage over one who looks dirty and yobbish. It is not supposed to make a difference but in a borderline case it just might.

Finally, acknowledge the value of sight by having on board some of the visual aids mentioned later in this chapter.

SOUNDS GOOD

At its most basic, this means that your car does not sound like a clapped-out old banger. Rattles, sputters or mysterious things rolling around in the boot do not help a prospect to relax! Eliminate any such noises before going on the first meeting.

How do you sound? Do you sound upbeat or downbeat, happy or sad, helpful or bossy? Ask your friends or partner for a no-holds barred appraisal of your speaking voice. If you have any verbal bad habits — lots of 'y' knows' or 'well basicallys', ask your helper to give you a kick each time you slip into them. With practice you can remove this annoying habit very quickly. (Think about your own meeting with such characters — after a while you stop listening to the message and start counting how many times the expression is used.)

Purge your vocabulary of 'thorn words'. These are words that make you say 'ouch' and think twice about what you are doing: 'sign', 'contract', 'appointment', 'cost' and 'lesson'. All words have other words that go with them and whether they register consciously or not they will start alarm bells going. For instance you 'sign' in blood, sign on the dotted line, sign your life away. An 'appointment' is something you have with a doctor or a dentist. Try 'Will you OK the paperwork' or 'meeting' instead. After a little thought and practice you will see how some words can explode like land mines. You should never, by the way, use words like 'sale' in front of a prospect.

It is not just the sound of your own voice that can be persuasive. Have you ever wished that you could have a prospect hear the delighted praise of someone who has passed with you using the same methods? You can if you want to, you know. Buy one of those little hand-held recorders, the kind used for recording memos or thoughts. The next time you have a pass, ask a favour.

Talk the excited new driver through his or her problems and how you dealt with them. Use leading questions to highlight any special features or methods. (Make a script for yourself, beforehand.) You may need several 'takes', but delighted students are usually willing to help.

Keep each interview on a separate tape labelled with relevant information ie, 'Novice Driver, Eighteen, Course' or 'Multiple Test Failure, Forty, Gears'. After a while you will build up a small library. Select the tape for the job before meeting the prospect and show how you were able to help someone just like them. Or rather, let your excited pupil speak on your behalf.

NICE FEELINGS

Compared to the lot of most salespeople doing a presentation, the ADI is living in paradise. Not only do you have a product which is exciting and is a legal requirement, you can enable your prospect literally to get hands-on experience.

Harking back to first impressions, think about what happens to your hapless prospect on a hot day. All that morning, lots of sweat, sticky hands have clung to the steering wheel for grim life, leaving behind a gelatinous ooze that could trap flies, if not kill them. Now comes along someone who might just spend some money — if he or she can tear his or her hands from the steering wheel, that is! Keep a soft cloth with you in the car and wipe down the steering wheel and seats before meeting with a new prospect.

A sticky wheel will not on its own make or break a sale. Compounded with other factors though, it just could. Do everything you can to make that first encounter as nice and pleasant as possible.

SMELLS ALL RIGHT

Unpleasant smells can really change the outcome of a presentation. The chief offender is the smell of stale cigarettes (see

Chapter 6, 'The Fatal Five, pp. 79–81). You should avoid smoking while teaching, full stop. You can wind windows down and take breaks but it will still linger on your clothes and in the car. Also you will lose non-smoking pupils, maybe one or two a week. Can you really afford to do that?

Likewise, avoid eating in the car. Your timetable should allow for a proper relaxing meal in any case, otherwise you will come to feel like you live in it. Let the car smell of polish and newness, not of burger and chips.

Carry with you gum or breath freshener for first meetings. It is a date, remember?

Finally, don't go from bad to worse. If you intend to use one of those hang up fresheners in the car, reduce its potency by letting it stand out of doors for a few days. That way it will smell nice without killing all known germs and your prospects besides!

THE INSTRUCTOR'S SALES KIT

You need tools for any job and selling is no exception. The sales kit below should be in your car whenever you are and should be checked as religiously as your oil or water. Some of the items you will use every day, others are more specialist items that serve as a back-up. Experiment and then practise until you feel comfortable. The items recommended are as follows:

- Briefcase.
- Presentation file.
- Quality pen.
- Coloured pens.
- Notepad.
- Pencil with eraser.
- Toilet bag.
- Envelopes.
- Calculator.
- Business cards.
- Hand-held tape recorder.
- Proof tapes.

- Change bag/phone card.
- Street guide.

Briefcase

A briefcase offers both practical and psychological benefits, the latter suggesting order and a businesslike attitude. This may sound silly, but far too many ADIs carry around piles of paper stuffed into carrier bags, which does not make for a good first impression!

The case lid can be used as a sort of desk, but be careful not to create a barrier with it (see In-car Body Language, Chapter 5, p. 66).

Finally, a word about contents. Don't overfill the case and don't keep your lunch inside. When you flip those catches it should be like a doctor or a scientist showing off vital instruments.

A Short Discourse on the Presentation File

A presentation file is not just a container to help you keep your paperwork in order. Used correctly it will help you to close sales you would otherwise have missed, and will give both you and your prospect a feeling of confidence.

Presentation files come in a variety of sizes and prices, and consist of a leather or simulated leather backing with clear plastic wallets inside. The better the quality, the better an impression you will make, so it is worth spending a bit extra on such an important tool.

Like your sales kit itself, the presentation file has various components. Its purpose is to show who you are and what you do and it should contain the following items:

- Company logo/licence.
- Pass of the week.
- Pre-prepared charts/displays.
- Sample course schedules.
- Sample teaching aids.
- Diary sheet.
- Test application forms.
- Appointment cards.

Company Logo/licence

A company logo or identity is well within the reach of every ADI these days. An exciting, coloured page is a great way of opening a presentation and helps the prospect to feel secure with his or her investment. Ask a friend with a computer to help or maybe even a prospect with one. Alternatively, refer to the companies listed in Appendix 4.

Coupled with this, you should have a full colour reproduction of your ADI licence in your file. Not only does this reassure the prospect, it can also form the basis of a sale. It works especially well against large schools which employ lots of trainees, most of whom will not make it to where you are now:

ADI:	This chap offering lessons at £3 an hour you've seen, is his licence the same colour as mine?
Prospect:	I'm not sure. Does it matter?
ADI:	Well, yes and no ... if it's a different colour then it means he's a trainee. Now there are very good trainees about, but he still won't have passed his finals. He may never pass his finals — the failure rate is shocking. You could turn up for lessons one day and find him not able to teach you anymore.
Prospect:	He never said that!
ADI:	That's probably why he's so cheap. It's up to you. If you're happy with a trainee ...
Prospect:	I'm not! I want the real thing.

Dirty, maybe; business, definitely!

Pass of the Week

Take some stiff, coloured card and write or print *Pass of the week* on it. Slide it into a wallet and then use the underside to put in the thank you letters that you are now going to collect.

Without a shadow of a doubt, every pupil who has passed with you has promised a letter of thanks and lots of recommendations. A few of them might even have delivered, but most will not. It does not mean that they are bad people, it is just human nature. For you to have both of these in the quantities you need you are going to have to take control.

The next time a pupil passes his or her test, whisk out your quality notepad (see below). Ask the pupil to write a letter on the spot while he or she is still excited. As with the tapes, you can prompt and advise as to key features.

Make your first letter undated. This will serve as your pass for the weeks when you don't have any. Try to get the other one as up to date as possible (it is not encouraging to a prospect to see that your last pass was ten weeks before!)

Using this method you will have a steady stream of proof letters. If the passed pupil is known to the prospect this will have an even more pronounced effect.

Pre-prepared Charts/Displays

In this wallet you can place colourful diagrams about learning methods such as those in Appendix 2 (pp. 129–135), or cuttings from newspapers. Newspaper cuttings have the added bonus of being true.

Sample Course Schedules

These are the real 'guts' of your presenter and will help you to bridge the gap from past to future with ease and style.

From among your records dig out a pupil who passed with you after just ten lessons. If you don't have such a pupil then make one up. The main thing is that the pupil seems real to you because he or she is going to figure in a story you must tell.

Let us call the pupil Meg. When Meg came to see you she was 24 with one test attempt behind her. Her failure was down to a combination of nerves and reversing problems. Prior to coming to you, Meg had only done weekly one-hour lessons and been put in for her test when she was 'ready', which seemed a long, long time.

After taking Meg out on a trial lesson you diagnosed her problems and prescribed a course of five two-hour lessons, with a test at the end. The story has a happy ending — she passed with flying colours and drives to this day. The trick now is to get the story in print.

Write (or better still type) Meg's story out on an index card. Put flesh on the bones with whatever details you feel appropriate. Include a test date and a *total* cost and make that visible.

The next step is to draw up a training schedule. Take a weekly planner sheet and block in five two-hour lessons and a test. In the lesson spaces write as legibly as you can what you would be doing ie, reverse parking practice. When the schedule looks good, use highlighter pens of different colours for lessons and test. Staple the story card to the sheet and insert the whole into your presenter wallet.

Repeat the exercise for 16-, 20- and 24-hour courses. Keep the problems and ages varied — make the pupil and the story real.

You now have an excellent set of visual aids designed to sell block bookings. They work on a similar case history basis, so try and match the appropriate treatment to the patient. When you hear complaints about the timings, take heart. This is called in sales parlance a 'buying signal' and means that you are almost there.

Sample Teaching Aids

Place in this wallet specimens of any printed material you intend to use — diagrams, theory test papers, etc. Flip through these quickly — the purpose is to sell, not to teach. You are out to impress the prospect with your in-depth system, nothing more.

Diary Sheet

This is included mainly as a practical aid, but it can also be used in selling (see below, Pencil with Eraser). Accompanying this should be a photocopy of a diary for the year in which you are working. To show how busy you are, put coloured lines through all the previous weeks. These will represent courses you have completed already. In the month ahead of the one in which you are working, strike out two other lines. You now have only two slots available for tuition. Would Sir like his course in the second or the last week of the month?

Test Application Forms

You should carry around a good supply of these. If possible, transfer the details that you have from your telephone enquiries sheet on to these prior to meeting the prospect. When he or she sees a half-completed test form it acts as a real spur to finish it off and book!

As mentioned earlier, do not let the pupil complete and post off his or her own test application. This practice invites trouble, so avoid it by taking control from the start.

Appointment Cards

Cement the deal by filling out an appointment card stating the day and time of the next meeting.

That's about all on the presentation file for the moment. There are a couple of other forms to be included, but these are dealt with in the next chapter. You can, of course, add whatever else you think fit, but keep in mind at all times that this is a selling aid.

Quality Pen

Not a pen but *the* pen. Have with you a pen that looks and feels good, one with which it is a pleasure to write. Such a pen will boost your own self-image and impress the prospect with your prosperity.

Avoid soggy and chewed pens at all cost. The pen can be used to control attention and lead the eye through diagrams, but one that is part-digested and sticks to the paper sends out the wrong signals altogether.

Coloured Pens

A set of coloured pens is essential if you want to sell with diagrams (Appendix 2). Choose stubby markers with vibrant colours. (Note: wind the windows down a little if using them a lot.)

Notepad

This item should be in the plural. Keep one for jottings and diagrams and a better quality one for use with client letters.

Pencil with Eraser

Believe it or not, this humble item can make you a lot of money. Here's how ... Prior to your first meeting with a new prospect, fill up next week's diary sheet with lots of pencilled-in clients (all booking two-hour minimum lessons, of course). Use whatever names you want, leaving gaps on two days when you want to be in that area of town.

As you attempt the close, the prospect will see how popular you are and be impressed. Instead of a brain-taxing question like 'When do you want to go?', you can offer a straightforward either/or choice.

If the prospect tries to stall or says that both times are genuinely impossible, then you have a solution. Explain that the pupil on their preferred date is retired and can go at any time. Rub out the fake client and insert the real one in *ink*, making great play of the new client's favoured status.

Toilet Bag

Whether you like it or not you will be judged by appearances in the first 15 seconds, so get it right!

Carry with you a comb, breath freshener, aftershave or perfume, etc. The prospect has to fall in love with you a bit or the sale is not going to happen. Logic is a poor seller, emotion a great one.

Envelopes

You will need envelopes for two reasons, which are: letters of thanks to prospects; and dropping messages off at clients *en route*.

Calculator

A calculator can be a wonderful help but use it *with* the prospect, not *on* them. Don't hunch up, muttering in a corner when they ask you how much; this is intimidating to say the least. You should know your course prices by heart, and they are what you are going to sell in the first instance.

If using the closes described in Chapter 8, hand the prospect the calculator. Make the prospect into a partner, not an object. For this reason select a big calculator with large keys.

Business Cards

You should *always* have business cards on you. If you try and eat regularly in places during your day's work you will be asked for them a lot. Instead of snatching a sandwich in the car, go in somewhere and let it be known to the staff that you are a specialist in solving driving problems. You will be amazed and gratified at how word gets around.

Recorder/Tapes

The use of these is described above. Do seriously think of investing in one.

Change Bag/Phone Card

Don't be scurrying around for change to put in meters or phone boxes. Remove this irritant by carrying around a little bag of change prepared the night before. A phone card is useful – the boxes are usually empty and you can give the dead card to your accountant.

Street Guide

You can make money with these too. Help a pupil to think of anyone within a circled area who he or she knows who might want lessons.

LAST CALL

The very last thing to do before going out to sell is to check that your prospect will be there for you to see. Some ADIs advise against a preliminary phone call on the grounds that it gives the prospect a chance to change his or her mind. Good. If a prospect is that weakly motivated you will not convert them and if by any chance you do then you will live to regret it.

Begin your call by introducing yourself, taking care that there is a smile in your voice. If you feel nervous about this just say that you are checking the address and whether the time is still OK. Remind them at this stage to have their licences, test fees, deposits or whatever, then say goodbye. *Do not* get drawn into a discussion about prices. Having said that, you will get an inkling of what sort of level to pitch the sale at from stray comments. Use your ears.

Ideally, you should call everyone before setting off and this includes existing pupils as well as prospects. Once again, there are those who say that this is impossible during a busy day. Which is easier, though, a 30 second phone call or a 30 minute drive across town to find nobody home?

5

THE SALES PRESENTATION

IGNITION!

You have checked the address, checked that the prospect is ready and willing and have arrived on time. The rest is a piece of cake. All you need to do is to give a top quality lesson, is it not?

If you go in with the above attitude then be prepared to lose about 70 per cent of your potential clients. The biggest mistake most ADIs make is that they try to teach prospects to whom they have not yet sold themselves. Prospects are not, despite what they say, all that bothered about what does what, goes where and how it is done during a first meeting. More important are the unstated questions on the other side of their eyes; who is this person, is he or she nice or nasty, am I going to be taken for a ride? If you start teaching before you have dealt with these key issues then you are wasting both time and money.

The first meeting is about selling yourself. You will, of course, need to incorporate some hands-on time, but it is vital to realise that it is only there to progress the sale. Identify the prospect's needs during a drive and then select a simple, easily corrected fault. Teach the correct method of doing this as a sample, but don't spend too long on it. Do enough to leave the prospect with a sense of accomplishment, but no more. Avoid the trap of making the sales presentation an apologetic 5-minute tail end; that way, all you will get for your pains is an 'I'll think about it'. Active selling begins the moment the client gets into your car and stops only after they have left it.

ICE BREAKING

Most prospects are going to be even more worried about this first meeting than you are, so try and put them at ease. Begin with a warm smile and fuss over the prospect as if receiving an honoured guest into your home. Help out speedily with any seat or belt problems — you are not training them just at the moment, so don't sit back and make them fumble. Get them out of sight of watching neighbours and friends then introduce yourself, preferably with your presentation file. From their response find out what they want to be called and stick to it punctiliously. If the prospect is formal then stick to Mr, Mrs or Ms (if they give you a first name then avoid any shortened versions as this may have unpleasant associations). Similarly, be guided by their actions with regard to shaking hands. Some people like it, some don't. With practice you will be able to judge if this courtesy should be observed. If you do, then make your grip firm and brief — not a 'bone crusher' but not a 'dead fish' either. And smile. Don't forget that you have only got 15 seconds to register as nice or not.

DISCOVERING MOTIVATION

After the ice-breaking stage you need to establish very quickly why the prospect wants to drive. This may sound silly, but if you find the right answer then almost every prospect that enters your car will leave it as a committed pupil. What you have to remember is that nobody really wants driving lessons, just as no one really wants a mortgage. In the latter case what the prospect wants is a home and the mortgage is the necessary evil that comes with it. In your case the prospect wants to drive for myriad private reasons. If you try to sell lessons at this point you will lose a lot of business. Sell dreams instead.

The ability to drive represents different things to different people. To a 17-year-old male it is almost a coming-of-age ceremony, giving freedom from parents and the chance of taking girls out, becoming part of the pack. To a woman on her own it is an escape from late night bus stops, from drunks and perverts. To someone in the jobs market it is about promotion or maybe a company car. To someone with a sick relative it is the ability to take them back and forth from hospital or out on little treats. These four simple examples contain really powerful motivating factors — sex, fear, greed, conscience. It is the same with everyone.

Find out what makes your prospect tick, his or her 'hot button' in sales parlance. Each and every moment they have their hands on the wheel feed the dream, the feelings back to them. For instance:

ADI:	Just think Nick, in a few weeks you'll be doing this on your own. How are you and your girlfriend going to feel then?
Prospect:	Great!

Or again:

ADI:	If you go for a short course, Wendy, you'll be able to get rid of all those late night bus journeys. Will that make you feel better?
Prospect:	Lots!

Remember, it is how the prospect *feels* that will decide the issue almost every time. We buy with our emotions and then use intellect to justify the action afterwards. If the emotions are fully involved then money ceases to be a problem except in the most genuine of circumstances.

Weave lots of 'feel-finding' questions into this first encounter and listen carefully for the feelings behind the answers. Keep in mind the sales adage about having two ears and one mouth, to be used in those proportions. Find the tiny spark of a dream inside each prospect and gently nurse it into a roaring flame. Do this correctly and you will not have to sell too hard at all. The prospect will be pressing money at you before you can get your order form out.

IN-CAR BODY LANGUAGE

Before and during the presentation, take careful note of the prospect's posture and gestures. These can often provide you with valuable insights as to what the prospect is thinking as distinct from what he or she is saying.

The study of body language or kinetics is a fascinating science in its own right and anyone involved in sales at least should master its rudiments. Within a car, of course, the 'vocabulary' that can be employed is much more limited than in some situations, but even so it can be a powerful selling aid.

Take, for example, a very simple method of registering annoyance or suspicion, tightly crossed arms. If you have a prospect adopting this pose then something is wrong somewhere, and all your honeyed words will not get you inside the prospect. The mind follows the body just as the body follows the mind. Before you work on the problem you must first pierce the armour that the prospect has put on for a fight or flight situation. This is relatively simple. Smile at the prospect and say 'You look really tensed up and angry — what's wrong?' Suddenly self-conscious, the prospect will open up those arms to reveal a vulnerable body and a vulnerable mind. They may even tell you what the problem is!

Hands straying to the mouth tend to be unconscious signals of a lie. If a prospect promises you this and that with such gestures then exercise a degree of scepticism. The gesture of rubbing the nose or scratching an ear signifies disbelief or dislike of what you are saying. Hands on knees or rubbing thigh tops points to a desire to be off. Study yourself and others in spare moments and take note.

On an even more esoteric plane is the subject of eye movement and thought, which also affects how we speak. All of us tend to be dominated by certain senses more than others and this in turn controls our mental pathways. Someone with a strongly visual nature, for instance, comes out with expressions like 'I see what you mean' or 'Look at it this way'. An auditory sort of person might say 'I hear you' and so on. The key to understanding what is going on inside someone's head is to be found in their eye movements, which indicate their type when a question is being analysed. If you can establish which mind set is dominant in a prospect you can use examples that he or she can assimilate.

Finally, those of you who wear spectacles can put them to good use. When a prospect is giving you a hard time, take them off in a slow, relaxed gesture. Suddenly you are disarmed and vulnerable and the prospect will soften. Try it!*

THE FACT FIND

Next in importance to discovering motivation is establishing what the prospect can afford and what his or her expectations are. You need this information long before you get to the sale and the best way of obtaining it is through an extended fact find. Most ADIs operate a fact find to check up on previous experience, driving problems etc; the difference here is that all the questions are sales oriented. You need to know:

- How much the prospect has paid for lessons.
- When the prospect wants a test.
- What sort of time the prospect has available.
- To what groups or clubs the prospect belongs.

Some of these details may be available through your telesales sheet, but work through it thoroughly. Intersperse technical questions with sales questions so that your strategy is hidden, rather like a doctor collecting facts for a diagnosis. Use this analogy if pressed and think on these lines. For instance, if the prospect

---

* The above is only a brief summary of what can be done; the ADI is strongly recommended to read the works of Robbins (1988) and Pease (1981) mentioned in Appendix 3.

wants to know why you need information about the volleyball team to which he or she belongs say this is because you want to note hand/eye co-ordination, not because you want referrals!

Get the prospect accustomed to seeing you write things down on forms. The idea is to normalise the act and so avoid the sharp intake of breath heard in so many presentations when it is time to sign up! Take as much information as you can, but offer no diagnosis or comment. Your purpose here is to pave the way for the sale, not to attempt the sale itself.

THE SALES PRESENTATION

The running order of a typical first lesson is this; icebreaking, fact find, driving assessment and then sales presentation. As mentioned earlier, it is useful to correct a *minor* fault to give the prospect a sense of accomplishment, but never lose sight of the fact that the sale is the objective.

Having finished the drive, pull over into a quiet spot. This should be well away from the prospect's home or drop-off point; get too close and the prospect will be itching to get out. (You can, of course, do the sales presentation in a cafe or the prospect's home, but be aware of the pitfalls. In the first instance the prospect has to adjust to a new environment; in the second, you do.)

With the car safely parked, help your prospect to relax. Let his or her heartbeat steady and look for signs of unease presented through body language. Begin your campaign by collecting lots of affirmatives and restating the goals that the prospect expressed ie, 'Did you enjoy the lesson?', 'Do you understand reversing better now?', 'Do you still want a test in four weeks?' and so on. Lots of little 'yesses' put together help to make the big one that you are after.

The above 'yes questing' strategy takes advantage of two important psychological principles. The first is that it is very hard to say 'no' after you have said 'yes' a number of times (assuming the answers were sincere, of course). The second principle involves deferred excitement. Think of a Christmas pantomime in which the screaming kids have to shout back at the actors, or a religious rally where tension is built up in stages. Everyone knows where the questions are leading, everyone knows what the outcome will be, but both audience and leader pretend not to. Why? Because human beings, like all animals, like to play. The relief that follows on from the last 'hurrah' is almost orgasmic.

Do not be in too much of a hurry to move in and close the deal. Present your alternatives which are:

1. A prepaid intensive course.
2. A minimum two-hour regular lesson working towards a test date.

Assume that you have the sale. Now you have got the prospect you are just helping the prospect to decide which way is best. This assumptive attitude, like uncertainty, is very infectious. Assume the sale has happened and in most cases it will.

Keep a little distance between yourself and your solutions – that way the prospect can attack worries without attacking you. It may be an either/or choice, but the prospect has to choose. You need to ask, not tell. Pepper your presentation with questions, eg:

- 'It's a lot better learning in a short time rather than in months and months, isn't it?'
- 'Don't you feel better working to a test instead of just drifting?'

Practise ending all your sentences with a question. It's very easy to do this, isn't it? Can you see how this will help you? What you are doing is allowing the prospect to sell themselves, aren't you? What the prospect says must be true, mustn't it?

The sale will go much better if you utilise a presentation file such as that described earlier, or visual controls like the diagrams in Appendix 2. The real secret is this, however; *know exactly what you and the prospect are going to say. Work to a script.*

This does not mean literally. You are not a mind-reader to predict the prospect's very words. However, you can predict the objections that will come your way and the words you will use in response to them. Stop reading now and write down the top objection that you get during the course of your working day.

The chances are that you have written 'cost' or 'money'. So what is your response? If you try and make it up on the spot you will lose out every time. You need to rehearse your responses. Try this one:

Prospect:	You're very expensive.
ADI:	I'm not expensive — it's everyone else that's cheap!

Back this up with something even more dramatic. Cut out from your local paper the section advertising driving lessons and highlight the £3 or £4 an hour merchants. Tell the prospect that you are not willing to work on a false premise. Your aim is not to make them a lifetime companion but to get them through their test quickly, and that involves burning petrol. So-called 'cheap' lessons invariably turn out to be more expensive in the long run but if that is what they want, well, you are prepared to help too. Offer them the piece of paper and urge them to ring around. Guess how many will?

Write down all the objections that have floored you in the past and work out a response to each. In general, all you need to do is back off a bit and lead the prospect through what he or she came to you for in the first place. Objections do not mean that the sale is off – the opposite is true, in fact, if you use them correctly. Objections are stepping-stones, nothing more.

The final stage of a sale is called the close. Usually this will involve obtaining signatures and asking for money. Remember, never ask a prospect to 'sign' — it is always initial or OK. The best place to get it is on the test form; few prospects can resist that. Asking for the test fee takes you smoothly into asking for a deposit or weekly retainer. 'Oh, by the way, I usually ask for ...'

You need to feel good about closing. It is not a question of pressure or brainwashing, it is just helping people overcome quite natural feelings in making a decision. The best ever definition of a close is that offered by Tom Hopkins (1983): 'Closing is the process of helping people make decisions that are good for them'.

In Chapter 8 you will find a collection of closes designed especially for driving situations. Learn each, role play it and use it together with others. If this makes you feel manipulative then think about it this way. The prospect is going to learn to drive with someone. If you, offering a good, fairly priced lesson, cannot or will not close because of erroneous moral objections, he or she will fall prey to someone who will offer the world for nothing. Who have you helped or protected?

I NEED TO TALK TO ...

Occasionally you will find the close frustrated by the prospect saying, 'Oh I need to talk to my wife/husband/dog, the President, James T. Kirk ...' (Shame on you for not finding out who the decision maker was during your fact find!)

It is not over till the fat lady sings, however. If a prospect says they need to talk to someone then smile and tell them no. Say, 'That's my job!' and try to arrange a meeting. If the significant other is in the house waiting, so much the better; if not, fix a time.

If this is a genuine situation and not a stall you will probably be welcomed with open arms. Take your presentation file and go through the entire sales sequence. Don't just present a price, provide explanations. This way nothing gets forgotten or distorted in transmission and you can walk out with a fully approved sale.

THE THINKING-IT-OVER PROSPECT

By following the recommendations above you should have happily converted most of your prospects. You might have missed something though, in which case you will hear a line you just might have heard before: 'I'll think it over and get back to you'.

Now the average ADI curls up and dies on getting that one. Calling the prospect thick, dense or claiming that you did not like them anyway is not the way to become an above average ADI, which is the goal you have set yourself. This is how to treat a prospect who wants to do some thinking …

Let us take a typical situation. You have just done a presentation on a client named Beth and she is not buying. The fact that you have heard the T word means that you have not found her motivation or dealt with her worries. Therefore you have got some work to do. She has promised to think, but life, soap operas and parties are going to get in the way. Days will pass and you will not hear. If you do chance to call back you will find out that she is driving with someone else who could get around it.

The solution is to look vanquished and offer a vague smile. This relaxes the prospect who then thinks that he or she has won; there is nothing to fear from a defeated salesperson. Begin by confirming that the prospect is about to do some serious ratiocination. The prospect will say yes because he or she will be convinced that the meeting is over.

ADI:	You're obviously interested, Beth, or you wouldn't go to the trouble of thinking it through, would you?
Prospect:	Oh, I'll give it some real thought, honestly.
ADI:	Can I ask something directly, Beth — you're not just saying this to get rid of me are you?

The prospect will be a little taken aback by this. If you have done your job well at all, most prospects will say that you are the best thing since sliced bread. Fine. That is one item thought over.

ADI:	Just to help clarify things, Beth, was it me or the lesson? Did I put too much in?
Prospect:	No, it was ever so good. I feel I've done hours.
ADI:	Was the early test a problem? Did I spook you a bit?
Prospect:	No, I need one real fast.

ADI:	Did the hours I advised for you to pass with confidence seem too many?
Prospect:	No, they're about what I thought.

This really is a case where 'no' means yes. Each time the prospect answers, he or she is confirming the good points of what you have to offer. Unless the prospect is asleep, he or she will see where this is going and seize on the real objection. Money. Show the prospect that you understand the reluctance to commit, that you empathise.

Prospect:	Actually, it's just what I want. It's the cost.
ADI:	So cash is the only real problem?
Prospect:	That's all.
ADI:	If I could show you a way around that how would you feel?
Prospect:	Interested!

There are two possible moves from here. The first is to go through the selling process again and prove that your tuition is more cost-effective. An easier method of closing the sale, however, is to determine just how many two-hour sessions a week they can afford and book them in an extended course. Use the training record sheet in Appendix 1 and fill in the weeks to the test. ('Are Mondays and Thursdays best or would you prefer Tuesdays and Fridays?') To secure the sale fully, obtain some extra commitment by asking the prospect to do homework on a non-driving day. ('You'll have to work hard to help me ...') Finally, ask for and obtain a retainer.

The above strategy is designed to get over the thinking-it-over stall. Pupils who are thinking it over must become a thing of the past. Go for a sale; if you get a no, at least it is better than a false and useless hope. A thinking-about-it pupil hardly ever comes back, so preserve your dignity by rejecting him or her first.

NEXT, PLEASE

Congratulations! You have just made the perfect sale and both you and the prospect have emerged from it as winners. A deposit is sitting in your case, you have got the test fee and form, life is good. Don't cheer too soon though, because there is one last thing to do that really will make it the perfect sale. That last thing is locating the prospect who will replace this prospect in the form of a referral.

Referrals can transform your business beyond all recognition. To see why they are so powerful look again at the sales cycle. Let us say your advertising is good and your telephone technique is better. Being the star that you are, you book five out of five. Each of these five prospects is unknown to you, and vice versa, which means that they will be preoccupied with questions they would never dare ask. Questions like, 'Who is this person?', 'Is he or she trustworthy?', 'Is this a rip off?', 'Will he or she laugh at me when I mess up?' You can rattle on about gears and such as much as you want, but they will not be listening so much as thinking. Now, unless you are very good at selling, you might convert only two of these prospects. That means that three of your valuable hours have produced little or nothing, and you have lost work that you could be glad of later. What if, however, those five hours were spent not with strangers coming in cold but with friends of pupils who have already passed with you? This time each prospect knows who you are, knows you are trustworthy, knows it is not a rip off and so on. The questions of cost and value will have been dealt with long before they get into your car. Booking them becomes almost a formality. In an average week you will convert three such prospects and in a good one five. The same number of hours have just made you twice as much money.

Working with referrals will do more than just improve your closing ratio. It can, for instance, improve the quality of your pupils. With few exceptions we all mix with our socio-economic equals. Someone with a good salary does not usually spend time with benefit claimants, so the names you get are likely to be able to afford you as well! Referral technique also allows you to pick pupils who are likely to need maximum hours eg, young drivers. Once again, like moves with like. Most 17-year-olds have friends who are much the same age, most of whom will want to drive.

Given these obvious advantages it is sad that ADIs do not pay more attention to referral gathering. By the end of year two, in fact, a competent instructor should be getting 60 to 70 per cent of new business in this way. To achieve these sort of figures some *active* prospecting is called for.

When the subject of referrals is mentioned most instructors smile thinly and say 'Oh, so and so who has just passed her test is going to mention me to all her friends'. That is not prospecting and that is not good enough. At best it will only result in a trickle of new names, and what you need is a flood. What is much more likely in this situation is that your delighted pupil will just forget. It is not that people do not mean to help, but life, cars, work and soap operas get in the way, as I mentioned earlier. The promise is lost and will never come back. Also, if you rely on passed pupils, you are only going to get a figure that matches your pass rate! That means that you lose the chance of getting new business leads from up to 50 per cent of the people climbing in your car. You simply cannot afford to do that.

The time to start asking for referrals is the first or second time (at the latest) that you have someone in your car. There are many useful methods of obtaining referrals but the standard ADI technique is not one of them:

ADI:	Do you know anybody who wants driving lessons?
Prospect:	No.
ADI:	Oh. All right then.

After two or three stabs like this most ADIs give up on the idea and write off referral gathering as something occult like selling, and that all pupils are hermits with whom even double glazing firms don't bother! It is hardly astonishing that prospects react like this when given such a question, however. What you need to do is paint pictures of the kind of person you want:

ADI:	Tim, I love helping people in your age group through the test. Has anybody else in your class got a problem with test dates?

That will not always get you names, of course. Sometimes you will have to work a little harder. There are two very powerful techniques: the credit card close (see Chapter 8, p. 105), and the test observation method (see Chapter 7, p. 95).

For now, though, let us stick to the basic request. As in the sale itself, you have to show the prospect why helping you is going to be a help to him or her:

ADI:	Tim, one of the reasons I can spend more time with you, as I have done today, is that I get nearly all my work from referrals, so I don't have to waste hours looking for pupils. If we could think of someone else I could help, I wouldn't forget you, of course.

At this point arouse the prospect's own self-interest. You might want to offer a free hour before test or something of that nature. When the prospect has warmed to the idea, go through likely associations — clubs, groups, work — and pick out names from each.

Another strategy, which you can dress up as psychological motivation, is this:

ADI:	Alex, which of your pals would you like to pass your test before?
Prospect:	Well, there's Nick who gives me grief about how good he is. Steve maybe. Why?

ADI:	There's two reasons. Obviously, if you pass first, you'll want to rub their nose in it.
Prospect:	Not half!
ADI:	Right. So what I'm going to do is prepare some 'I've passed with an Instructor' cards for you to send out.
Prospect:	Brilliant!
ADI:	The other thing is it will help your confidence a lot if you believe you'll pass ... How about you bringing your address book to the next session? We'll let your ten favourite people know you've arrived before them!

Of course, you do not want to wait until the prospect has passed (he or she might not anyway!).

So, next prepaid session, when the prospect appears with his or her address book, you will have something else extra: a letter of introduction.

Work through the names provided (on your time, not the prospect's) and gather as much detail as you can about each one. Name, number, job, test attempts — the more the better. And then:

| ADI: | Alex, I've a favour to ask. I've got a few letters of introduction for these friends of yours when they don't pass! There's a space for you to put on any comments about my style. How about it? |

The letter of introduction needs a brief, punchy message that says who you are and what you do. It also says that you are going to contact them by phone in the near future to discuss how you might be able to help them. Get your prospect to scrawl a few comments and initial it. If at any stage the prospect seems nervous, switch tactics and ask if, instead, you can just mention his or her name. You now have some valuable information. The rest is down to your phone technique.

If you master referral techniques you will never go hungry. When work is lean you can go looking for it and be certain that you are talking to real prospects, not just people who look in papers. Appendix 3 lists some excellent books with sections on this topic – try these variations out until you find the ones with which you are happy. You will soon have a minimum of five new prospects in your car each week. From there it is almost impossible to fail.

6

AFTERCARE

THE CARE AND MAINTENANCE OF THE PUPIL

'Look after your customers and they will look after you' is a dictum by which all salespeople must learn to live. Many ADIs, however, seem to think that they are an exception to this rule, and the result is thousands of pounds of lost business each year. You are in a competitive service industry and if you do not service your pupils correctly then someone else will. There are a number of simple measures that you can introduce to ensure pupil loyalty, but in the first instance it is vital to understand why so many leave.

THE FATAL FIVE: COMPLAINTS ABOUT ADIs

Excluding topics outside the remit of this book relating to poor technique (shouting at pupils, touching female ones etc), the most commonly heard complaints about ADIs are as follows:

1. My instructor always moves lessons or does not show up.
2. My instructor is always late.
3. My instructor always cuts lessons short.
4. My instructor is spinning things out.
5. My instructor smells like an ash tray.

If any of these complaints apply to you then read on; if not, move to the next section.

My instructor always moves lessons or does not show up. This grumble possibly has the most justification from the ADI's point of view. We live in an imperfect world and even the most carefully laid plans can go wrong. If that is the case and it is a rare error, no problem. If it happens on a regular basis, however, then you need to look at your diary control again. As was said earlier, either you run your diary or it runs you.

If you do have to move lessons for, say, a test or illness, then let your pupil know well in advance and sweeten the pill with a freebie. Never move a new joiner — move existing pupils. That way you will not run the risk of doing one hour and losing 24.

My instructor is always late. Lateness is again a symptom of poor diary control. Allow time for delays or roadworks and then add a few minutes on to the figure you have arrived at. If you are running late then phone the pupil before it becomes a problem. Don't leave the pupil simmering and building up a grudge.

My instructor always cuts lessons short. You do this at your peril! You may think that you can shave a few minutes from lessons and get away with it, but pupils soon notice these things; and change instructors.

Deal with any tendency of this sort by charging a retainer and seeking payment in advance instead of chasing poor quality business. If that does not make you give full value for money you should be looking for a new job.

My instructor is spinning things out. The fault here can be traced to a lack of confidence in prospecting and selling skills. In the vast majority of cases you should set a test date the minute you begin teaching and get on with a structured programme. If you have a good and continuous throughflow of prospects you will not need to ration the information you give out.

My instructor smells like an ash tray. This one really should not need any comment and yet it does. Your car is your workplace, your office, your stage, and it should not be polluted. If it is, and you only lose one prospect in five because of that, then think how much it will cost you over the year. It is an expensive and thoughtless practice that shows no courtesy.

Make your car a smoke free zone. Exercise the same control

over your students as yourself — they will not be able to smoke on test, will they?

DEALING WITH DIFFICULT PUPILS

Grumbles go both ways, and many are the ADIs who complain about 'difficult' pupils. There is a simple answer to this problem; get rid of them quickly! A pupil who finds excuses for not paying, a pupil who skips lessons or wants you as a taxi service is a pupil you do not need. It is not just the effect that such students have on your finances, it is the damage they can do to your morale and enthusiasm. Remove them!

You will find that the pupils who cause you the most annoyance are those from whom you will make the least money. The reverse is also true. It makes sense, therefore, to concentrate your energy where it will do the most good. You are not a social worker or a therapist. You are in business to earn money.*

Weed out potential stress-mongers by insisting on payment in advance in the form of a retainer or a deposit. If they will not agree to do so then you are better off without them.

SELECTIVE HEARING

A frequent source of conflict between pupil and ADI is just what was said at the first meeting. This is especially the case where 'extras' are promised — second test fees, free hours and so forth. No matter how scrupulously you present such things you will always get pupils who apply selective hearing. They pick up bits they like — usually 'free' — and tack this on to what they have imagined or hoped they have heard. When the pupil comes to collect his or her extras and discovers that they are not what he or she thought, the pupil will inevitably call you a liar or worse.

If you intend to offer things of this nature then put them in

---

* Don't fall, either, for the prospect who has left his or her money behind. Never offer tuition without first taking the cash.

writing. State what you aim to provide in clear, unambiguous terms and read it through with your prospect at the point of sale. By spending a few minutes in this fashion you will save yourself a world of trouble later on.

The above exercise of telling prospects what you *do not* do can also, paradoxically, become the basis for a very good sale. This is when you find yourself up against the so-called 'guaranteed pass'. In most cases this is a classic piece of selective hearing, but the prospect who has got this idea fixed in his or her head can be hard to shake. The other school the pupil has seen, he or she insists, will take him or her out forever for free until he or she passes!

Help the prospect see how impossible this position is by introducing some figures. The average test failure rate is around 50 per cent, so if an instructor has four pupils on test, then two will fail. That means that in week one, Mr Bountiful is taking out two pupils for nothing. In week two he will be taking four, in week three six, in week four eight — pretty soon he will be working for nothing!

If you go through this example most sensible prospects will realise what is going on and book with you instead.

CONTINGENCY FUND

Don't win a battle and lose the war. Even if you can prove with razor sharp logic that you are right and the pupil is wrong, think about the next sale and the next after that. One irate client can cost you more money than it takes to settle the dispute by bad mouthing you to all and sundry.

Money is usually what is required to put things in order if the car breaks down or if you are forced to miss lessons prior to the test. Don't argue, just pay. If you have followed the advice earlier about retainers then you should have an adequate contingency fund which is self-replenishing. If, in spite of this, the ex-pupil complains then talk about it openly with new prospects who might have heard. Once you tell them that the client got his or her money back they will agree that you were entirely fair.

THE 'THANK YOU FOR YOUR TIME' LETTER

After dealing with all the negatives, it is time to move on to positive measures aimed at keeping pupils on the books. Begin literally the minute they have left your car. Using your quality notepad, write them a short letter thanking them for the hour. If you closed them, assure them of your best services; if they said no, or the code version (I want to think about it), say how much you enjoyed meeting them and wish them the best for the future.

When the letter arrives, most prospects will be taken aback. Those that have not booked will be impressed by your attitude and will bear this in mind should things go wrong with their alternative choice.

MAKING MONEY FROM RECORDS

You don't have to sell vinyl to make money from records. Although most ADIs recoil in horror from paperwork, it can add greatly to your profits. All you need to get established are a couple of small index card boxes and a couple of packs of cards to go in them.

Make out a record card for every prospect that you take out in your vehicle. This should contain:

- Name.
- Address.
- Telephone.
- Workplace.
- Date seen.
- Hours required and cost.
- Motivation for wanting to drive.
- Driver number.
- Notes.

The completed cards are to go into your call back box. In this, place 12 cards marked with the months of the year, which will act as dividers. You will then need a series of cards marked 1 to

31 for each day of the month. Insert these behind the month card in which you have started your box ie, if you are commencing in October put them into November.

The next step is to put the pupil record cards into the system. Let us say that you take a prospect out on 14 October and she says that she wants to think things over. Most likely, this is a rejection, but the prospect is not lost to you yet. Put the record card for the pupil into the corresponding day of the next month. Your prospect will probably now be under instruction with someone else, but not necessarily happy with the choice so, in fact, there is a better than 50:50 chance that she may not like her new tutor as much as you. She is not about to ring up though and say come back, all is forgiven. For that to happen you will have to help.

On the appointed day, ring up the prospective pupil, with the card and all that useful information in front of you. Take a cheery, assumptive tone and say that you are making a courtesy call. Ask how the driving is going and if the prospect has passed yet. If the prospect seems happy then let it go and put the card three months ahead. If, however, the prospect is not fully settled, then do some positive listening. Resist the temptation to rubbish your competitor or go into selling mode; you have bridges to build first. The conversation might go something like this:

Prospect:	But he says I'm nowhere ready yet, so I haven't put in for a test, which is a let down.
ADI:	It is, I agree. I had some students start the same day as you and their test is next week, but I was lucky. What you've got to bear in mind though is that it will be quite a time from your application, so that might add another six weeks on.
Prospect:	Can you get me one quicker?
ADI:	Let's see, I might still have your driver number ... I could give them a ring tomorrow and see what's what.
Prospect:	Frankly, I don't think I'm getting anywhere at the moment.
ADI:	How many lessons have you had so far?

Prospect:	Six.
ADI:	That's handy. The big problem you had with the course I recommended was the price, wasn't it?
Prospect:	It was a bit more than I'd planned.
ADI:	Well, we can deduct those lessons you've done so far, which should bring the price down a lot. If I can organise you a quick test that might just be ideal for you! I could pick your test fee up — would afternoon or evening be better?

The secret of making call-backs is not to overplay your hand. You need to listen to what your prospect is telling you. Be like a patient fisherman waiting for the float to dip. When it does, strike — straight into your competitor's Achilles' heel.

You will not recover all your prospects this way, of course. However, even if you only get back 20 in the year, how much is that worth?

THE FUTURE BUSINESS BOX

This box is identical in structure to the call back box. Into it you should place details of all those pupils who have passed their test. Assuming you did not sign them up at the time for motorway, night or bad weather driving, now is your chance to do so. Build up a fine collection and, when times are lean, go back and sell the idea. For parents of young drivers this sort of thing makes an ideal gift.*

You can keep these cards longer for another sale. Who is to say that a year later your tame broker might not be able to offer a better insurance deal?

---

* Motorway sessions and night driving should be sold *immediately* on completion of a successful test. As the pupil jumps around for joy, fix them with a steely glare and say that you want to see them next week for two hours. When they ask why, tell them it is to keep them alive a bit longer — it is a good close!

EXOTICA

There are various learning aids which can be hired out to pupils. This helps them to achieve their goals and also generates small but welcome amounts of cash. Included under this heading are motivational tapes, videos, and books. You can buy these or make your own. Two very inexpensive methods to use are:

1. To ask the pupil to pick up a picture of the car they hope to drive and look at it daily.
2. To create a series of flip cards. These are cards with messages typed on them which have meaning for the pupil ie, 'When I pass my test I'll be able to get a new job'. The pupil needs to look at these daily so that the motivational message sinks into the subconscious mind.

CONCLUSION

There is no point having lots of prospects if you are going to lose a large percentage of them. Learn to avoid the fatal five by tidying up your operation and you will make more money from fewer hours.

7
REPAIRS

THE CARE AND MAINTENANCE OF THE INSTRUCTOR

The most important tool you have in your quest to make money is not your car, it is you. Like a car, though, you have limits and a need for regular maintenance if you are to perform at your best.

The car analogy has one other thing to offer, and that is detachment from self. You are aware that your car is not part of you and therefore can examine its faults and problems with ease. Examining your attitude to life or personality without ducking the serious issues is more difficult. Constructive fault-finding requires that you stop defending your position and look at yourself with the eyes of a stranger.

Bodywork

Your first check test needs to be your physical health. Yours is both a stressful and a sedentary occupation, and you should keep this in mind. Your working week should include exercise, recreation and plenty of rest time; if you are controlling your diary then you will be working sensible hours with planned spaces for leisure.

Coupled with the above you ought to have a very clear picture of what happens if you break down. As a self-employed person you will not find yourself flavour of the month with the State if you need its help. A broken leg, an ongoing health problem – things that would be difficult for a salaried person are disasters for the self-employed. The onus on you is to sort this out for yourself and smartly. Like any kind of insurance, you will not be able to get it when you need it.

Make sure that any payments you have (car or mortgage) are covered by sickness and accident insurance. Generally these take care of your payments for 12 months. To protect yourself from longer-term problems there are other kinds of policy you should consider. Consult your bank or financial adviser. You will doubt-less wince at the premiums but put things into perspective by real-ising that it will only involve the profit from a single lesson each week. You will get your money's-worth in days if you need to claim.

Performance

Fortunately, physical conditions do not normally put ADIs off the road for good. Emotional and mental problems relating to the job, however, are another matter. If you find that you hate your occu-pation because of a lack of money, lack of hours or overwork then you have some serious thinking to do.

The root cause of most of the difficulties experienced by ADIs can be traced back to one thing and that is poor diary control. As stated in Chapter 2, either you control your diary or it controls you. Feast and famine cycles, lack of prospects, awful cash flow, they are all consequences of how you use or misuse time. If life is becoming a long series of grimaces then repeat the planning process you carried out earlier. From a clean sheet of paper rein-vent your working week. Generally speaking the place you should start is with obtaining lots more new prospects; you will be amazed at how much better you will feel with hordes of pupils suddenly appearing on the books!

Once a year (or half-yearly if you are having problems) you will need a major overhaul. The best way to achieve this is to take an hotel day.

Leaving the phone and all your worries behind, disappear for the day. Don't leave a contact number except for your nearest and dearest — for a few hours you are going to be unavailable. Find yourself a quality hotel in a peaceful setting out of range of every-body you might know. You will need a diary, a year planner, lots of paper and cash for a well-deserved lunch. Situate yourself in a lobby where there is a constant but not distracting business hum and go to work.

Begin by reviewing what progress you have made since your last planning session. Take a clinical rather than a critical approach. Your aim is to examine, strengthen and build, not to do penance for your sins. List what you have and have not done without further comment. Remember to include in this the non-material longings you identified in your original planner.

After a break or stroll, start work on your new targets and aspirations (some of these may be carry-overs from the previous exercise). As before, subject all your thoughts to the PRAMKU test. Weak resolutions will only end in failure.

The final phase is to write down the methods that you are going to use to make your dreams come true. Quantify everything as far as you can. Extend this principle to other than financial situations; if you are unhappy in your work or with a relationship, what are you going to do about it and when ?

Hotel days offer a chance to study your performance, restate your goals and recharge your batteries. Their most precious quality is that they provide something we give ourselves far too little of these days — the chance to think.

In the Garage

Just now and then you will find yourself confronted by a situation that seems unfathomable. If, after trying everything obvious, you still cannot find an answer, then it is time to seek outside advice. Try talking to a prospering ADI (pay for his or her time, of course). Alternatively, seek out some of the books in Appendix 3, or make use of the personal coaching services listed in Appendix 4. If none of this helps then you have got a real problem on your hands. You have got a slump.

HOW TO SURVIVE A SLUMP

Ask any sales professional about a slump and he or she will pull faces and describe the 'Mother of all slumps' in the most colourful and graphic language possible. It sounds, and is, a terrible experience but it is also a part of life like disease or accidents. You may be lucky and never undergo such a trial, but then again you may not. If the waves seem to be closing in over your head the remainder of this chapter may just save you from drowning.

A slump is the result of losing control of your business activity. This may be dependent on external factors such as illness or relationships, or internal ones such as disillusionment or demotivation. The longer a slump continues, the harder it is to distinguish between cause and effect. When you are negative and downbeat everything will go wrong and that, in turn, will breed further misery and so on. You must break the chain if you are to come out of your tailspin. It is either that, quit or go bankrupt.

First Aid

The flippant answer to surviving a slump is never to get in one in the first place. There is an element of truth in this in so far as the planning process should have kept you on beam, but none of us is perfect. The real solution is a 'blood transfusion' of new business to get you off the critical list. Presented below are methods of putting money in your pocket very quickly, which will go a long way to restoring your confidence. Before you start, however, apply some bandages. If a company or bank is chasing you for money, then approach them in writing with a compromise of reduced payments. Seek the help of local advice centres or debt counsellors. Take the heat out of the situation so that you can concentrate on the real business.

Back from the Brink — Mind and Heart

To pull yourself back from the brink is going to take a tremendous amount of courage and honesty. In the first instance you will have to lose some of the mental and emotional baggage you are carrying. Burn the past and forget about injustices, thankless friends and pupils. Begin with small, achievable steps and take it from there. Remember the sales dictum, 'It's a cinch by the inch, a trial by the mile'.

Flash Cards

These are a variation on the cards mentioned in the previous chapter for training pupils. Once again, it is all about feeding the subconscious mind with powerful, upbeat images that eventually will permeate all the way through your working day. As you replace negative ideas with positive ones, the difficulties that have been crushing you will just come to look like problems to be solved by hard work. That is all that they are really.

Take 20 index cards of a colour that appeals to you. Next, think of power phrases that really make you feel good about your business and reinforce your self-esteem, eg, 'I get so many referrals that I've more work than I can handle' or 'I teach only quality pupils'. Type rather than write these messages on sticky labels and affix them to the cards. Between appointments or whatever, shuffle through the cards and soak in the messages.*

The Dreams Scrapbook

Commence your mental housekeeping by making use of the creative power of visualisation. Replace miserable, useless images with small but happy dreams that you can turn into realities.

Buy yourself a cheap scrapbook, the kind you probably had as a child. Next, cut out pictures of some items that you want. They don't need to be expensive in the early stages; it could be clothes, a book, a CD or whatever. It is important that you get a picture from a catalogue or magazine though. Put one picture on each page and write down a target to be linked to it, eg, 'I will buy this CD when I see ten new prospects' and so on.

---

* Keep the cards in a plastic bag or box. Replace at once any that become tatty or dog-eared.

Leaf through the book at least once a day, more if you can. The minute you hit your target, get the treat you promised yourself and tick it off, then go to work on the next.

After a while, both your targets and your rewards will get bigger. It is then that you can include pictures of cars, houses and holidays and really enjoy the fruits of your labours.

Make Yourself Lucky!

Sometimes you will get to feel that all you need in life is a little luck. That may well be true, but it certainly is not going to come to order. In actual fact the reverse is usually the case — when you need it most the wheel of fortune will turn somewhere else and leave you fuming.

You cannot make yourself lucky but you can make yourself *feel* lucky, and after a while one thing leads to another … It may be an old fashioned concept but count your blessings daily and revel in how lucky you are. And you *are* lucky if you think about it. If your health is good and you are at peace with yourself the rest is just window dressing.

On a more mundane level, give yourself the chance to be lucky. Garages, shops, magazines and so on often have free prize draws which involve nothing more than sticking your name in a hat. Forget the lottery — that builds up too many illusions and costs money. Go instead for little things that you have probably ignored till now — make it a sort of hobby. Even if you don't win, the emotional reward will put spirit back in you and make you lucky for real.

Generate Enthusiasm

Lastly, and most importantly, you need to generate some enthusiasm. Enthusiasm, like depression, is infectious. If your mood is enthusiastic then the people that you meet will be swept along by it. It is very hard to say 'No' to a sincerely enthusiastic person.

Relight the fire that took you through Parts One, Two and Three. Stop watching the televised news with its non-stop sewer of misery, fear and hate and start your day off with something more positive. Play motivational tapes, read a favourite book or maybe just listen to the birds sing. Whatever it takes to make you enthusiastic about life, do it! You must transform yourself from the party-goer who sees a half empty glass into the party-goer who sees a half full one.

Practise enthusiasm even when it hurts. Like everything else it is a question of habit. Keep up a buoyant, eager front for long enough and it will cease to be a front. At that stage, you are ready to begin some practical work.

INCREASING YOUR ACTIVITY LEVEL

Having dealt with your emotional problems it is time to look at practical measures. The way out of a slump can be summarised as this; increase your activity level. If you see enough prospects then everything is gong to come right very quickly.

In the midst of a slump your diary will be full of gaps. Good – this means you have lots of time to see new prospects. Interspersed with meeting lots of eager prospective pupils, you are going to earn some money!

First of all, prepare the ground. Get a month's supply of new business activity forms (Appendix 1) and resolve to use them religiously. Even if you have to start with lots of noughts, grin and bear it. Within the space of a few days it will inspire rather than depress. Moreover, it will allow you to prove to yourself on paper what has gone wrong.

Old Business, New Business

A good place to begin looking for instant work is with your previous pupils. If you've been keeping the call back boxes mentioned in the previous Chapter, then this is easy. If not then go back through your records and try out the suggested script. Set yourself a minimum number of calls each day and record these on your activity log together with the outcome.

Mock Tests

The mock test can be used as a money-spinner as well as part of the teaching process. In this instance you are trying to capture prospects who are not your pupils to generate some simple, no complications cash.

Take out a line in your most productive newspaper. Try something like *Mock test and report only £19.99*. You don't want many details — keep it tantalising and short. The prospects you are looking for are either under tuition and nervous or so over-confident that they have dispensed with lessons altogether. Your mission, simply put, is to give them hell.

Be very clear about what you are offering here. The deal is a fixed-price session designed to replicate test conditions. If you get extra hours from it then so much the better, but what you are looking for is volume. These prospects will not be tested under your auspices, so you need have no fear of adverse comments from senior examiners or the like. You are there to generate fear, and for once any lack of people skills just could be a bonus! The pupil's reward from this exercise is a taste of things to come — your reward is quick but honest cash. Once you have explained who it is for (experienced drivers or those awaiting test), sell it over the phone like this:

Prospect:	I can drive really well, but I go to pieces on the test!
ADI:	That's very common and also very natural, so don't feel too bad about it. A lot of people who fail the test go down through nerves, not lack of skill.
Prospect:	That's me.
ADI:	Do you remember the first time you took a lesson with an instructor? You probably felt really self-conscious about that as well — it's the new pair of eyes that does it.
Prospect:	I could hardly start the car!
ADI:	The trouble is, whoever takes you out ceases to be a threat. It doesn't matter whether it's a friend, a relative

	or a proper instructor, after a while you get used to them. They lose their shock value. And then the examiner gets in ...
Prospect:	Don't remind me!
ADI:	What I'm offering is an hour of nerves! You've never met me, and if all goes well you'll never see me again! I'll put you through a mock test that'll make your hair stand on end — no mercy, eh? At the end of it though, you'll feel much stronger and used to being watched. And you might just pass this time.
Prospect:	What's the catch?
ADI:	None. At the end of it I'll give you a report with my comments but the rest is up to you.
Prospect:	When can I go?

If you come up against a prospect who has paid out lots already or who is with someone else, add the following sequence:

ADI:	Actually, Mr Prospect, the best way to think of this is to see it as an insurance policy protecting your investment. You've already spent several hundred pounds learning to drive — it would be a shame to waste it all just for a few quid, wouldn't it?

If the prospect fails, guess who he or she will be coming back to?

The Test Observation Method

A related technique of prospecting that works with a pupil already under instruction with you is the test observation method. This exercise genuinely helps students to come to terms with their nerves and at the same time feeds lots of new prospects into your business. Moreover, it does not cost a penny!

The Driving Instructor's Guide to Effective Selling Skills

As an existing student approaches the test date, remind the student of the biggest problem he or she faces. The dialogue might go something like this:

ADI:	Liz, we've done everything we possibly can. I think you're up to test standard or I wouldn't recommend you sitting. The only thing that will shoot you down is nerves on the day.
Prospect:	I know! I'm sweating already!
ADI:	That's understandable. I've heard lots of people say the same and still pass. There is something else we can do, though. If I could show you a way of coping with nerves would you help me with it?
Prospect:	I would. I really need to pass.
ADI:	What happens on a test is that all of a sudden you've got a new pair of eyes on you. It's not that the examiner is a monster, it's just somebody different. You probably felt the same the first time I took you out on a lesson, didn't you?
Prospect:	A bit.
ADI:	Now, though, you're not scared of me and that's the trouble. I want to give you a serious mock, but without some fear it's a waste of time. Do you have a friend who'll give up an hour to help you out?
Prospect:	How do you mean?
ADI:	What I want, Liz, is a friend of yours to sit in the back while I do your mock test. I don't want them to say anything, I just want their beady little eyes boring into the back of your neck. How's that sound?
Prospect:	Horrible! If it'll help though …
ADI:	The thing is, Liz, we need your friend to be a non-driver. Someone who knows how it would do more harm than good with tips and advice. We want someone about your age with no history. This is really important for you, Liz, so think hard.
Prospect:	Well, there's Cath …

ADI:	OK, if you could talk to her before the next lesson. We can pick her up *en route*.
Prospect:	All right then.

Like any good sale, the above sequence represents a win/win situation. The pupil now has the chance to experience some nerves — if the pupil needs convincing further then tell him or her that it is like having an inoculation to ward off a disease. When you have the agreement tied up, get the friend's name, address and telephone number for 'insurance purposes'.

You now have a very highly qualified lead in the back of your car. On that day, of course, you are going to give the most dynamic session of your life. Your pupil's friend will be taking all this in and perhaps making a decision. In a way it is better than a free lesson or trial because it puts no pressure on the prospect whatsoever. If you fail to get a booking then put the details into your call back box and ring him or her in a few months.

Intensive, of course

The last thing you need to do now that you are running again, is to book an intensive course. Re-read all the relevant sections and go out to sell some. At this stage you will have time to use the credit card close (see Chapter 8, p. 105) so do so! The date may be a couple or more weeks away, but that does not stop you asking for a 50 per cent deposit, does it? Does it?

CONCLUSION

The above techniques are designed to get you out of a hole very quickly. Use them to stabilise yourself and then take control!

8
CLOSING TECHNIQUES

CLOSING WORDS

As discussed earlier, a close is a group of phrases or ideas designed to help the client to reach a positive decision (by now words such as 'sale', 'buy' or 'argument' should be well and truly absent from your vocabulary). The close is the one thing that stands between you and the living death of all salespeople, the 'I'll think about it' line. If you close correctly you will hardly, if ever, hear that dreaded phrase.

The very best closes are those which help the client to realise the value of their decision with little or no help from the salesperson — they are mental hooks on which your prospect hangs up all his or her worries. Just offer the box of chocolates and then sit back. There is no need for the so-called 'hard sell' or bullying tactics. You do not sell; the client chooses.

Listed below are a variety of closes tailor-made for use in a driver training situation. Each of them encapsulates an idea that helps the non-driver or novice driver to relate the experience to something more familiar. They all work. The trick is to select the right one for the situation and use it effectively.

Read through the closes and make sure you understand the principle involved — any uncertainty will lead to confusion and close *you* down. With the idea absorbed, flesh it out and make it your own so that you can slip it into the conversation with 'spontaneous' flair.

The next step is to practise the close on a friend or partner. As always, invite constructive criticism and be big enough to accept it. A tape recorder or a video camera will be extremely useful in this exercise.

The final stage is to try it out in the field. A thorough knowledge of your prospect is the key to selecting the appropriate close. It is a little like picking the right golf club or screwdriver for the job in hand.

You can, of course, use more than one close in a presentation. Be careful not to overburden your prospect with images, however. Then they really will need to go away and think about it!

Each close also contains a secret method of doubling your business activity within weeks. All you have to do is put it into practice.

THE CLOSES

1. The Cost of Delay Close

A thorough fact find is essential to make this close work. As the prospect threatens to 'think about it', ask him or her to work out the cost of delaying a positive decision. Take daily bus or train fares and multiply them by the 20 or 30 weeks required for conventional tuition. Don't forget to add on visits to friends, family, days out, etc.

If the prospect is capable then involve them by handing over the calculator while you make notes. Coupled with the mounting figures, this sense of doing rather than being done to makes for a very persuasive close.

When you and the prospect have arrived at a final figure, write it down. Contrast this, in a different colour, to the cost of your week or month course to show how much money can be saved.

The secret technique to double your business within this close is obvious, is it not? They probably sit next to someone just like them every day on the bus or train. Ask for referrals.

2. The Tennis Close

A close that could equally well be called the football close, rounders close etc, this sequence is designed to help you bunch lessons together for maximum profit and commitment. Explain how the human body is programmed by reference to a sport, eg, when a tennis ball whizzes towards you at 90 mph, Mother Nature says 'duck'. To play tennis you have to reprogramme the nervous system so that instead of flinching you hit the ball back.

Compare the above example with learning to drive — speak in terms of new reflexes for distance, speed, gear changes and so forth. Finish with a smile and a reference to popular folklore about practice making perfect. Especially concentrated practice.

The secret method for doubling business? Ask for referrals.

3. The Taxman Close

This is an excellent close for a situation in which your prospect is the son, daughter or spouse of a company director and works for that company (as is often the case in small businesses). Explain how the cost of training a member of staff who also happens to be a member of the family can, in certain circumstances, be set against tax. Ask the decision maker whether he or she would like the taxman to pay half the bill for lessons and see what follows ... This close travels well by word of mouth. Ask the prospect if he or she knows of any other small companies which might benefit from this angle.

4. The Antibiotics Close

When a prospect fights shy of committed, intensive training ask if he or she has ever had a course of antibiotics. When the prospect answers 'yes' in a puzzled voice, explore the reason why the recommended dosage has to be taken at the recommended time. (In case you don't know, it is to keep a certain level of the drug in the bloodstream. Miss doses and the offending bacteria may well develop immunity.)

Liken the driving lessons you have recommended to this example. If the prospect takes just the odd lesson now and then it

The Driving Instructor's Guide to Effective Selling Skills

will not help his or her 'condition'. In fact, bad habits will develop resistance.

Does the prospect have any friends in need of treatment? Ask!

5. The If It Is Good Enough For Them Close

This close is used to sell intensive courses. Explain how bodies such as the Armed Forces and large companies use this method to train their people to drive. Such institutions have all the time and the money in the world but they still choose this system. If it is good enough for them is it not good enough for you?

This close works very well with young males, who identify with the glamour image it provides. Don't forget to ask them if they have any equally resolute friends.

6. The Times Table Close

A close that can be used with very good effect on multiple test failures. Liken the matter of bad driving habits to a child learning the times tables. If a child gets 13 x 9 wrong then he or she can repeat it a thousand, a million times, and it still won't come out right. So it is with driving skills. Unless a fault is corrected mere repetition is useless; what is required is a burst of concentrated training followed by practice.*

7. The Marathon Close

Use this close on a disaffected pupil still waiting for a test date from a reluctant-to-part-with-money type of instructor. Compare his or her present situation to a marathon runner who does not know where the finish line is and so is not certain whether to sprint or stand still. If the pupil is not aware of when the test is after so many lessons, when is he or she going to find out? You, of course, will book the test date the minute the pupil has given you the go ahead and a deposit.

---

* Pick numbers that will cause the prospect to think hard. This will reinforce the teacher/pupil situation and lend you status.

When you ring later to inform the pupil of the good news, you ask the pupil if he or she has any friends in a similar situation.

8. The Later Than You Think Close

Test requirements are changing constantly, and who knows what the coming months or years will bring? One thing is for sure — the driving test is not going to get any easier. Nor, for that matter, will lessons go down in price, inflation cease or petrol get any cheaper. When confronted with a prospect who will not make a decision in case it is the wrong one, help him or her along with a glimpse of things to come.

Do they have any friends who need to get a move on?

9. The Package Holiday Close

If a prospect tries to push for an aimless hour a week session, ask him or her a simple question. Would he or she book a package holiday without knowing the cost, how long it was for or when the flight was? The answer is invariably a laughed no, at which point you ask why learning to drive should be any different. Instead of an open-ended commitment you can offer known costs and a proper schedule — that must be better than just going on and on and on.

Don't forget to ask for referrals!

10. The Week Or Month Close

A simple modification of the either/or questions you should always utilise. Take the prospect by surprise and ask whether he or she would like to drive in a week or a month. (The numbers can vary according to what your fact find has revealed about financial status, but offer two concrete and believable choices.)

A couple of referrals would round this close off nicely.

11. The Pass Rate Close

Only use this close if you have a higher than average pass rate and you can prove it! If your prospect says that price is the only obstacle, help him or her to put things into perspective and on paper. Ask just what the lower rate they had in mind is and jot it along-side the competition's pass rate. Most prospects will not have a clue about this latter figure, at which you should raise an eyebrow and say that the average pass rate is around the 50 per cent mark. Quoting your own test pass rate, ask if an extra couple of pounds is worth a 20 per cent or whatever advantage.

At the risk of becoming a bore, ask for referrals. Do they have any friends who would like to increase their chances of passing?

12. The Week Challenge

Best used on the overconfident prospect who has 'been driving for years, know what I mean?', this is a dare as much as a close. Such prospects grossly overestimate their own prowess and resent paying for lessons they 'don't need'. To land them, take them out on a very full lesson, but don't argue your case. Instead, invite them back at the same time the following week for a mock test. When they realise that they have forgotten most of what you showed them they will come along quietly on a short intensive course.

This sort of prospect always has plenty of mates in the same fix. The only question is, do you really want to ask for their names and numbers …?

13. The Emergency Drill Close

Compare the prospect's learning situation with that of a jet fighter pilot undergoing emergency drill training. The pilot repeats the drill time after time after time until it becomes second nature. When a crisis happens for real, the pilot's mind goes blank for an instant just like anyone else's. At that stage, however, conditioned reflexes take over and result in action. Liken the moment of panic felt at test and explain how concentrated lessons will get the prospect over that moment.

Do their friends need this sort of action?

14. The *Queen Elizabeth* Close

When a prospect disputes the amount of lessons recommended, help him or her to think the situation through. Confidence is one thing, risk taking another. Explain how even a luxury liner like the *Queen Elizabeth* carries life boats just in case. The extra hours you have advised are like those lifeboats. Contrast the slightly extra cost with the emotions experienced on failure.

Has the prospect any friends or colleagues who would enjoy some straight-talking?

15. The Taxi Meter Close

Designed to sell two-hour lessons, this close will also help you to overcome 'cheaper' competition. Use it only on people who have had a sprinkling of lessons, however; a total beginner will not understand what you are talking about. Compare an hour lesson to a taxi ride in a taxi where the meter runs backwards. You may begin with 60 minutes, but unless you or the tutor is an android, quite a few minutes will be lost on pleasant chatter. Next, mirrors and seats need to be adjusted. All this time the clock is tick-tick-ticking. When the driving begins maybe 20 or 30 minutes more is spent on repeating the last lesson. There is hardly any time left for something new!

Do they know anyone else getting taken for a ride in a taxi with a backwards meter?

16. The Credit Card Close

This close can take up a lot of time and so should not be used when you are busy. On the other hand, it is a great way of putting dead hours to good use and digging yourself out of a hole.

If the pre-closes have worked well and the client seems to be on the verge of making a decision, offer to get the test sorted there and then. Ideally, go back to the prospect's home and, armed with his or her credit card or yours, pick up the telephone and sort out a booking. Involving the prospect at all times, set the deal in stone. While the prospect is still on a high, ask for your deposit and start working the hours backwards.

Before you leave, ask if they know anyone else who would benefit from this service.

17. The Shallow Pool Close

Liken one hour a week training to drops of rain falling to make a shallow pool. Within no time at all the pool gets dried up because it is not deep enough to survive. Deeper pools do, though. In driving instruction terms one-hour lessons are like stray raindrops that do nothing but evaporate, concentrated lessons are like deep water that can be put to use.

There is not really an obvious referral line on this one but ask anyway.

18. The Cost of Living Close

Use this close on older prospects or the parents of new drivers. As they protest about the cost of lessons, ask them how much they used to pay for lessons. The figure is going to be laughable but, as you will point out, so were wages. Let the prospect work out for him or herself what percentage of his or her pay driving lessons accounted for then. In nearly every case you will be able to show that the price of lessons has gone down in real terms. When the prospect or parents realise it is not such a rip-off they will usually pay without further dissent.

Ask for leads.

19. The For/Against Close

Commonly known in America as the 'Benjamin Franklin', this simple yet elegant close works by encouraging participation and seemingly handing over control of the decision-making process.

Present the prospect with a clean sheet of paper. Use a thick marker pen to divide it in half and on one side write *for*, and on the other *against*. Explain that this is a scientific analysis to see which form of training would suit them best ie, hourly or a condensed course. Ask the client to list the advantages of a course – prompt, but do not tell. The comments must come from the client in order to carry conviction.

The next step is to list the disadvantages of such a course. Usually there will be only one — price.

The client is now in full possession of all the details he or she needs to reach a decision. Don't labour the point, however. Help rather than sell. You can say that the exercise has identified all the problems and that a logical analysis shows which is best. If money remains the only problem try extending the course into easier to afford units (six weeks, ten weeks etc).

Do they know anyone else who would benefit from such a scientific approach?*

20. The Old Banger Close

Just occasionally, you might end up driving a car that is less than impressive. You will then live in fear of the competition's hot wheels or, even worse, the prospect who says 'I'm paying out how much an hour for *that*?' Don't despair, however. Even within this fraught situation there is a wonderful close — if you have the humour and confidence to try it.

Your reply to the insulted prospect might go something like this:

> Mr Prospect, as you've noticed, my car isn't exactly new – it's seen life, you might say. The thing is though, it's just a tool like a hammer or a saw. In order to make its product — that's you — a qualified driver, I expect it to take some punishment.
>
> Now if you go out with someone who washes his car three times daily and all but takes it to bed with him, it's going to be a long time before he *really* lets you drive. You might scratch the paintwork or upset his little darling. As far as I'm concerned though you're here to learn how to drive. Unless you wrap us round a tree or something, I'm not bothered too much what you do to the *tool*. We can get some good driving going. Do you want to worry about breaking eggs or make an omelet?

---

* Use buzz words like 'scientific' and 'logical' frequently in this close.

21. The Two For The Price Of One Close

Explain how traditional one hour a week driving trains the mind but not the body. Most pupils who take and fail their test know how to drive mentally but not physically — they lack the conditioned reflexes and responses that will allow them to concentrate on what is going on outside the car instead of in it. No wonder, then, that so many fail.

Your condensed method, however, trains both the mind and the body. You may be a little more expensive than some, but in reality you are training two people not one. That makes the cost very competitive.

Ask for names of friends and workmates.

22. The Baking A Cake Close

Another close designed to sell short courses that will benefit both the prospect and your cash flow.

Compare learning to drive to the process of baking a cake. You can put in all the ingredients but unless you have the right temperature the attempt will not succeed. In this case the 'heat' is provided by putting lessons close together.

23. The Champion Close

Simply ask the prospect if he or she has ever heard of anyone who became a champion snooker player by practising one hour a week and leave them to draw their own conclusions.

Ask for referrals.

9

THE ROAD AHEAD

This book opened with a number of challenging statements and it will end by repeating them. The first of these was that, in a very real sense, technical ability is of less consequence in making money than sales ability. Nobody has better skills, better breaks or better pupils, the only 'X factor' involved is how an ADI functions as a salesperson.

The second assertion was that work for the ADI is both plentiful and controllable. Life does not need to be a series of boom and bust cycles, months of plenty and months of starvation. Your working day can be as structured as that of any employed person's in a nine to five environment. The question is, are you willing to abandon familiar patterns of failure and try something new?

The road ahead for you as an ADI is as smooth or as difficult as you choose to make it. Good sales and planning skills will remove most of the uncertainty and pain from your working life. Take, for instance, the matter of unsociable hours griped about by ADIs and (more often) by their partners. There is no reason in the world why you should be grafting while everyone else is playing — in actual fact there are good reasons why you should not be that impact on the pupil. You work odd and uncomfortable hours because traditionally that is how it is. You can change this if you want to. All you have to do is sell the benefits of your action to the prospect, eg:

ADI:	Terry, it's like this. I can take you out at 7 or 8 pm or Sundays , but that isn't going to help you with your test. Your test will maybe be at 8 or 9 in the morning and believe me the traffic flow will be *very* different.
	Now some instructors will just take your money and let you take your chances, but I'm not like that. I want you to pass.
Prospect:	So do I!
ADI:	You need everything in your favour, Terry, and learning to drive in an artificial setting is a dead loss. Can we look again at this, even if it means waiting till you've a few days off work?
Prospect:	Well …

Note how this is done for the benefit of the *prospect*, not because you and your partner deserve to enjoy life like any other human being. Don't be afraid to ask prospects to make an early start or to take time off work. They want to pass more than you, remember. Ask for what you want in the proper way and you will get the right answer more often than you would think is possible!

LIVING IN PARADISE

As an ADI you live in a salesperson's paradise. Your product is exciting, sexy, useful, necessary and legally required. You could not ask for more, you really couldn't. So if you are not happy but in a nether world of despair then you need to recognise what the problem is.

There is not, and never will be, a shortage of work. Prospects are to be found everywhere, but what you make of them is another matter. A pupil should be for life, not just for a test! Most ADIs throw away lots of business because they don't understand this; they are like gold panners who throw still glistening raw material back into the river for want of an extra shake. The value of a pupil begins with theory training then practical training, moves on to post-test tuition, insurance, warranties, etc, and above all referrals. If you organise things correctly a pupil can provide you with income years and years after his or her actual test.

NEW OPPORTUNITIES

Following on from this are the new opportunities afforded by changes in DSA policy or requirements. Passplus, for instance, is something that you should make conditional for almost every pupil. If you cannot sell it to the prospect through the carrot of cheaper insurance, then sell it in life-saving terms to spouses or parents. The key word is sell.

Even more exciting in financial terms is the introduction of the theory test. The simple measure of setting up your own local centre can do a lot, from reducing the number of hours you need to work to bringing in new prospects. Forget any reservations you may have about group teaching and get on with it. See it as your 'Part Four' and go into action.*

DIAMONDS IN THE ROAD

The Cat's eyes you see stretching ahead do not have to be Cat's eyes, they could just as well be diamonds. There is a sales story about this too, of course, and it goes like this ... In the dark and distant past, a Persian farmer became obsessed with the idea of a country rich in diamonds that he had heard about. He sold off his land, left his work and his family in search of his dream but found nothing. After years of sweat and bitter toil he died a pauper, lost and forgotten in a land of strangers. Just after his death, though, someone started to dig on the land he had abandoned at home and found it to be full of diamonds.

Are you willing to look for the diamonds in your own back yard?

---

* The companion volume to this, *Theory Training Skills for the ADI* will show you how to make this a really paying proposition.

APPENDIX 1
YEAR PLANNER AND FORMS

THE YEAR AHEAD ... THIS IS YOUR BUSINESS

Whether you are operating on a franchise, working in a partnership, or acting on your own, it is vital to recognise that you are running a business. Just like any other business you need to make plans. You need to know how much you can earn, what your goals are, what pitfalls may be awaiting you. For each year you work you need a new plan.

You can, of course, choose to work without any understanding of what it is you do. Don't be surprised though, if you are controlled by events rather than you being in control of them.

SELF-ASSESSMENT

Just what are your strengths and weaknesses as an ADI? Use this exercise to list the good and bad points of your selling self and what you might do about the bad. Help is available in the form of books, tapes and training companies, but first you must establish what you need.

Competency	Good	Fair	Poor	Action
First meeting				
Icebreaking				
Assessment				
Sales presentation				
Handling objections				
Closing				
Lesson planning				
Diary control				
Referrals				
Price competition				
Deposits				
Motivation				
Telephone skills				
Bolt-on sales				

NON-WORK RELATED OBJECTIVES

List below any ambitions you have that are *not* work related. These might include moving house, relationships, holidays, etc. Whatever your dream is, write it down!

_____

_____

_____

_____

_____

_____

_____

_____

_____

_____

_____

_____

_____

_____

_____

_____

_____

WORK RELATED OBJECTIVES

List below any work related objectives you have for the coming year. Do you, for instance, want a new car or to upgrade your ADI level? Write down, also, any operational areas you would like to improve eg, referral gathering, closing skills.

_____

_____

_____

_____

_____

_____

_____

_____

_____

_____

_____

_____

_____

_____

OUTGOINGS

Use the table below to work out your *minimum* financial requirements per week and month.

Item	*Per week*	*Per month*
Mortgage/rent		
Electricity		
Gas		
Water		
Tax/National Insurance		
Property tax		
Loans		
Car repairs		
Petrol		
Food		
Pension		
Insurances		
Clothing		
Office		
Other		

HOW I WILL ACHIEVE MY TARGET FIGURES

Now that you have established your minimum target figures, you can begin to put together a realistic strategy to achieve them.

My target figure per week is £—————————————————

This will be composed of:

	Hours	*Cost per hour*	*Total cost*
Trial lessons	_____ @	£_____	£_____
Prepaid course hours	_____ @	£_____	£_____
Motorway lessons	_____ @	£_____	£_____
Night driving	_____ @	£_____	£_____
Video hire	_____ @	£_____	£_____
Theory tuition	_____ @	£_____	£_____
Passplus	_____ @	£_____	£_____
Car insurance commission	_____ @	£_____	£_____
Other	_____ @	£_____	£_____

Total hours = _____

Total (Cash) = _____

YEAR PLANNER

The next requirement is to create a year planner for the year ahead.

Use the year planner to establish how many weeks you have available in which you can work. Strike out holiday times *now* if possible; this will both motivate and help you to budget.

Remove days that you do not intend to work ie, Sundays and deduct a further ten days for sickness. Add these numbers together, subtract from the days in the year and you have the real time available to you in the year to achieve your target figures.

Now repeat the exercise with the weekly work sheet. Decide first the hours that you are *not* available. Also, make sure you write down a list of things that have to be done every day (see Things to Do sheet). Using the methods shown in this book you can still make good money and have time to play!

Year Planner

January

Sunday	Monday	Tuesday	Wednesday	Thursday	Friday	Saturday

February

Sunday	Monday	Tuesday	Wednesday	Thursday	Friday	Saturday

March

Sunday	Monday	Tuesday	Wednesday	Thursday	Friday	Saturday

April

Sunday	Monday	Tuesday	Wednesday	Thursday	Friday	Saturday

May

Sunday	Monday	Tuesday	Wednesday	Thursday	Friday	Saturday

June

Sunday	Monday	Tuesday	Wednesday	Thursday	Friday	Saturday

July

Sunday	Monday	Tuesday	Wednesday	Thursday	Friday	Saturday

August

Sunday	Monday	Tuesday	Wednesday	Thursday	Friday	Saturday

September

Sunday	Monday	Tuesday	Wednesday	Thursday	Friday	Saturday

October

Sunday	Monday	Tuesday	Wednesday	Thursday	Friday	Saturday

November

Sunday	Monday	Tuesday	Wednesday	Thursday	Friday	Saturday

December

Sunday	Monday	Tuesday	Wednesday	Thursday	Friday	Saturday

Work Sheet

Work Sheet ....

Week commencing ....

Time	Mon	Tue	Wed	Thu	Fri	Sat	Sun
7am							
8am							
9am							
10am							
11am							
12							
1pm							
2pm							
3pm							
4pm							
5pm							
6pm							
7pm							
8pm							

EMERGENCY STOP!

If you found yourself unable to work tomorrow because of a broken arm, what would be the effect on your finances?

Do you need, or have you got, the following safeguards:

1. Mortgage protection.
2. Income protection.
3. Contingency fund.

If you do not have (1) or (2) consult the companies listed in Appendix 4 or your broker.

If you do not have (3) then use the retainer method to create one at once.

MY GOALS ARE ...

Draw together all the decisions you have made about your life in the previous sections and *write them down*. Continue on another sheet if necessary. Sign and date the contract you have made with yourself and get it witnessed by another person if appropriate.

Goal   *Target date*

LAST WORDS

Your business does not have to be spiralling out of control or little more than a glorified taxi service. Like any other enterprise it is responsive to planning, effort and discipline. Seasonal factors, pupil numbers, the hours that you work, referrals – everything that matters — is in your hands.

This is *your* business and it will be whatever you choose to make it.

Intensive Training Schedule

Pupil ....   Start date............................   Test date ....

	Mon	Tue	Wed	Thu	Fri	Sat	Sun
Week 1							
Week 2							
Week 3							
Week 4							
Week 5							
Week 6							
Week 7							

Client information sheet

Name:................................. Tel (Home):...........................

.... (Work):...............................

Address: ....

....

....

Pick-up point if different:..

Day: .... Date: .... Time: ....

Reason for driving: ....

Previous lessons:..

Price paid: ....

Test needed by: ....

Reason for changing ADI: ....

Notes:

_____

_____

_____

_____

New business activity log W/C:

Activity	M	T	W	T	F	S	S	Notes
Standard referral request								
Test observation request								
Letters of introduction sent out								
Business cards presented								
Leads from centres of influence								
Call backs to prospects who declined booking								

Total requests: _____
Total leads obtained: _____

Notes:
1. Record every attempt to obtain leads regardless of the outcome. If you do not ask then register a zero.
2. Use the blank spaces for any other methods of which you can think.
3. Complete this sheet every day for a week, then a month. Within a short space of time the figures will look very good indeed! All you need is persistence.

Things to do

Date	Target date	Tick when complete

Write it!   ...... don't try to remember

APPENDIX 2
SELLING WITH DIAGRAMS

Human beings are highly visual creatures who absorb as much as 85 per cent of the information about them through their sense of sight. Although many ADIs acknowledge this fact in their teaching practice by using diagrams and pictures few, if any, apply it within a sales situation.

Utilising diagrams in a sales presentation will improve your closing ratio dramatically. In addition to making full use of the above principle the technique offers several other advantages. First, it gives the prospect somewhere to which to 'escape'. The narrow confines of a car and prolonged eye contact can lead to discomfort and a feeling of pressure. A colourful or interesting diagram allows for a breathing space by providing a welcome diversion. Second, things to look at and discuss encourage a feeling of involvement. Finally, if the prospect has not encountered this approach before, he or she will find it new and exciting. This might just tip the balance in whether they take lessons with you or go to someone else.

Visual material can be handled in a variety of ways. Finished, high quality charts and diagrams can be placed in your presentation file and talked through. This method gives your demonstration a very polished and professional look. These days anyone with access to a computer can create stylish aids. Alternatively, you can have your own made to order for a small cost through the companies listed in Appendix 4.

The other method of employing diagrams is to create them as you speak. This lends your presentation real 'weight' and suggests both a scientific and individual approach. As you talk about problems the solution magically appears in front of the prospect's eyes. If you decide to use this method, then observe a few simple precautions. Remember body language in the way you position yourself; and use thick marker pens with negative and positive colours. (Don't forget to wind the windows down on a hot day!)

Practise using your diagrams until it feels natural to do so; the latter usage, in particular, really takes off when it seems spontaneous. Try inventing your own, too. Seeing is believing.

THE LEARNING CURVE DIAGRAM

Use this presentation to help your prospect choose an intensive course of lessons instead of hourly sessions with no financial commitment.

After determining the prospect's requirements take out pen and paper and begin thus:

ADI:	OK Miss Prospect, after looking at your hand-eye co-ordination, ability and so on, I reckon we can get you to test standard in 20 lessons. How does that sound?
Prospect:	Terrific!
ADI:	Glad you think so. There's a couple of ways to achieve this depending on how you feel. Let me show you what I mean (*draw, black marker*):

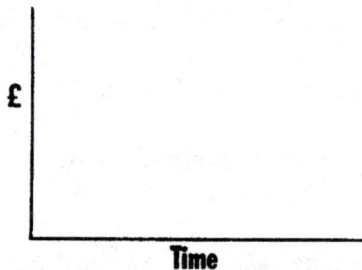

ADI:	This is a graph representing time and money. What happens when people learn to drive is that they do just one hour a week (*draw line on as below in black to build diagram*).

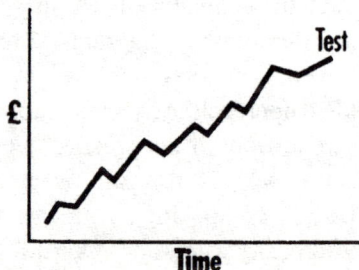

ADI: Doing it this way you learn, forget, learn and then forget again. The whole thing is a series of peaks and troughs. Of course, you always start off with a higher trough, but it's a very artificial way to learn. Did you ever hear of a tennis champion who won by practising for only one hour a week?

Prospect: Not that I know.

ADI: A far more effective and scientific way of learning to drive is to take a short course. Learning to drive this way irons out the peaks and troughs — it becomes a real learning curve (*draw in red as below*).

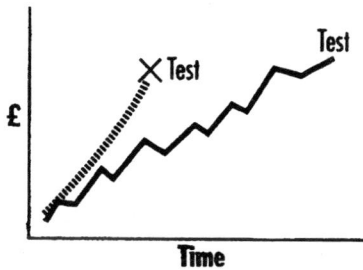

ADI: This means that you reach your goal much more quickly and you save all this time and money (*draw as below*).

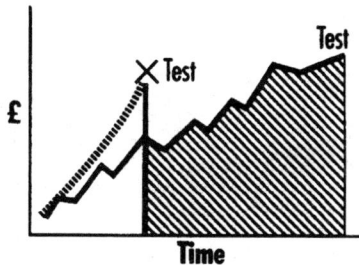

ADI: Which way do you prefer to learn, this way or that?*

---

* Those among you who are still awake will observe that the presentation ends with an either/or choice.

THE BRICK WALL DIAGRAM

This presentation is aimed at the prospect who has been 'driving for years, know what I mean?' During this time the prospect will have developed myriad bad habits, but usually he or she will be totally averse to spending money on wasted lessons. In order to explain what has happened you may have to use some 'concrete' imagery!

ADI:	That's great Mr Prospect! Like you said, you're almost there already! The thing is, though, you've picked up a few bad habits on the way. You were right; lessons would be a waste of money.
Prospect:	Eh?
ADI:	Let me show you what I mean (*draw as below*).

Foundation

ADI:	It's as if you've been building a wall with really solid, excellent foundations — that's the driving you've done already. The trouble is over the years one or two bricks have gone awry (*draw as below*).

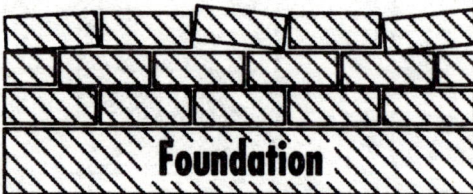

Foundation

ADI:	No matter how many bricks you lay after this has happened the wall is still going to be unstable. It's exactly the same in driving terms. The more driving you do, in fact, the worse things will get.

ADI: What's needed first is some demolition work. We need to get back to those good solid foundations and correct the underlying faults. Then we do a quick rebuild!

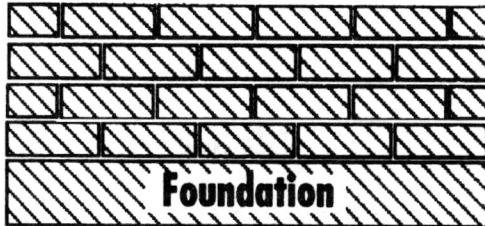

NB: In demonstrating this you do not have to strive for artistic perfection. So long as the diagrams follow your speech and turn words into pictures they will do the job.

THE 0–60 DIAGRAM

This presentation can be adapted to a number of situations but perhaps its best use is in dealing with 'cheaper' lessons. Establish the figure that the prospect has in mind (£10 in the example shown) and then draw a circle.

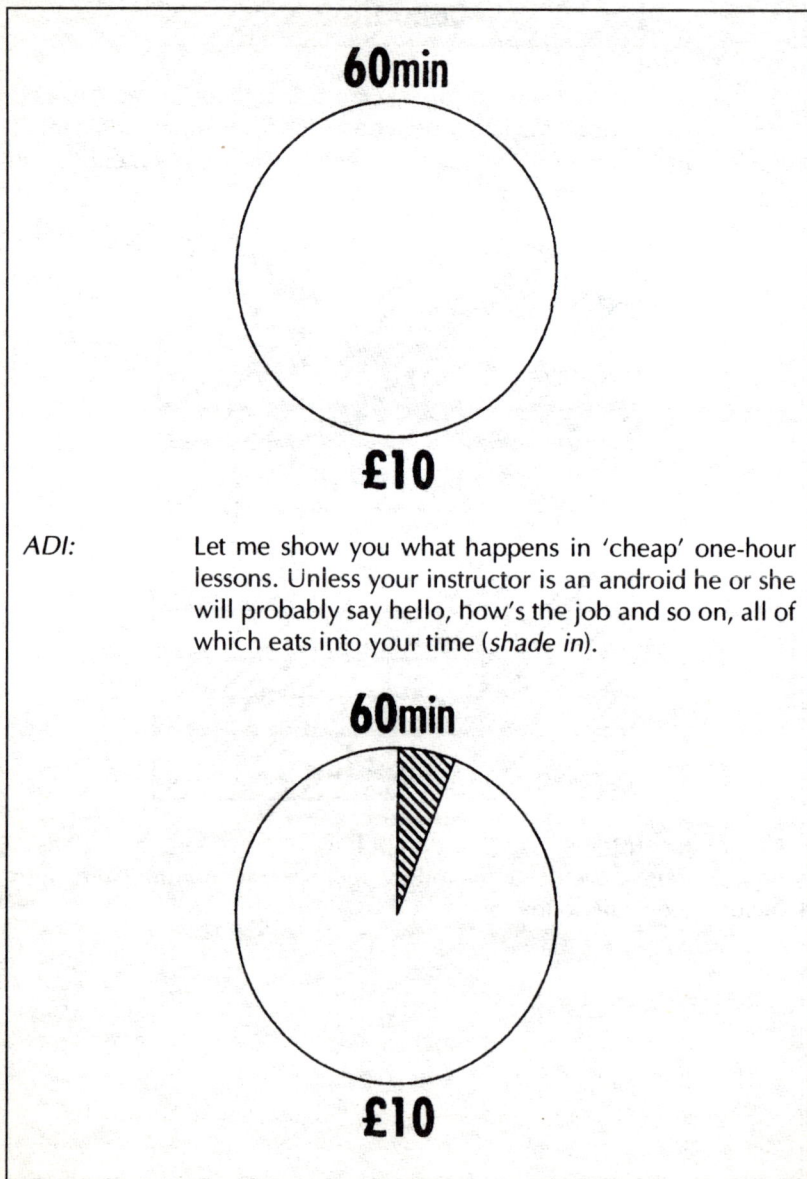

60min

£10

ADI: Let me show you what happens in 'cheap' one-hour lessons. Unless your instructor is an android he or she will probably say hello, how's the job and so on, all of which eats into your time (*shade in*).

60min

£10

ADI: The next thing is adjusting mirrors, seat and so on. More time lost (*shade in*).

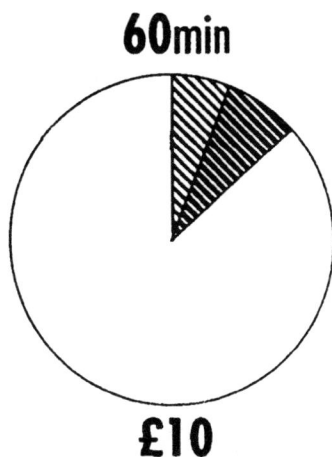

60min

£10

ADI: It's then that the real problem begins. The next 40 minutes or so will be spent on repeating the lesson of the week before. That means that the time for learning new techniques is under 20 minutes and, if you want to look at it that way, the cost per hour isn't £10. It's £30 (*draw*).

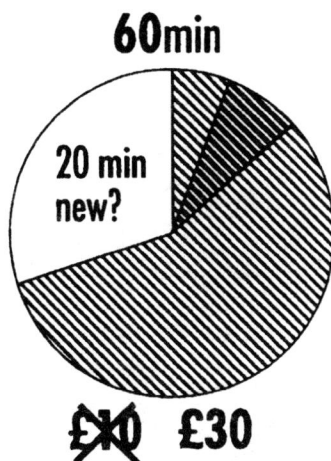

60min

20 min new?

~~£10~~ **£30**

Which do you think is better value, Mr Prospect?

APPENDIX 3
RECOMMENDED READING

There are literally thousands of books available on selling skills and related areas of self-improvement. Aim to read as much of this sort of material as you can. If you only get one good idea from a book and that one idea enables you to make a sale then your effort has been rewarded handsomely.

Make time in your schedule for a self-study hour. Get a drink, get comfortable and start to read. No matter how experienced you are, there is always something new to learn.

The following texts, listed in a very subjective order of merit, are highly recommended.

How to Master the Art of Selling
Tom Hopkins, Grafton Books, London, 1983

Buy, beg, borrow or steal this book! The cover states that this 'is the best book ever written on selling and salesmanship' and for once it is not just hype. Hopkins covers the sales cycle from start to finish with wit, elegance and dignity. Ideas seem to leap up from every page, together with practical measures that can turn any business around. Essential.

Power Selling: How to Realise Your Sales Potential
Michael Freidman and Jeffrey Weiss, Thorsons, London, 1989

A strong, well-presented study with short, highly motivating chapters. Very, very useful.

Selling to Win: Tested Techniques for Closing the Sale
Richard Denny, Kogan Page, London, 1988

One of the better recent books on sales technique. Nicely presented and thought out, it is a compact but very powerful text. (The pocket reminders it contains are worth the price alone.)

How to Close Every Sale
Joe Girard and Robert L. Shook, Piatkus Books, London, 1989

The title says it all. You will either love or hate this one but whatever your opinion, it deserves to be taken seriously. Like them or hate them, the authors are masters!

How I Raised Myself from Failure to Success in Selling/How I
Multiplied My Income and Happiness in Selling
Frank Bettger, World's Work, 1995 reprinted by Mandarin Press, 1955

These two volumes were practically the Old and New Testament for an entire generation of life assurance salesmen, and with good reason. Don't be put off by its background — selling life assurance is little different from selling driving lessons when you get down to it. Written with enthusiasm, frankness and compassion, this is the ideal book to help you out of a slump. Everyone in sales should read it at least once.

Cold Calling Techniques that Really Work
Stephan Schiffman, Kogan Page, London, 1988

Before you ask what this has to do with driving lessons, let me tell you. In the first place, either you, your partner or telesales are going to get phone enquiries, and this is the book to help! Second, there is the matter of all those call backs and calls you are going to make to sell night-time lessons, motorway lessons, insurance etc; and, more importantly, cold calls to referrals. Not so much a book as an investment.

Body Language: How to Read Others' Thoughts by Their Gestures
Allan Pease, Sheldon Press, London, 1981

As discussed earlier in this book, the 'vocabulary' of body language used in-car is curtailed by space. Despite this, you should be able to interpret gestures and mannerisms during the sale. This is even more important if you wish to move forward into the area of theory training for groups.

Wealth 101: Getting What You Want, Enjoying What You've Got
John Roger and Peter McWilliams, Thorsons, London, 1992

It cannot be said often enough that *you* are the tool that makes the money, not the car. If you get damaged —that is to say, demotivated, depressed, cynical or bored — then you really are in trouble.

Wealth 101 is an effective repair kit for the ego. In addition it is full of quotes from all sorts of people that you can try out on your prospects!

Unlimited Power
Anthony Robbins, Simon & Schuster Ltd, London, 1988

The mother of all self-help books! Use this text to explore and realise your potential by reprogramming yourself. The information on strategies for determining personality types is worth its weight in gold aside from any uplift you might get yourself.

The Driving Instructor's Guide to Teaching the Theory L Test
Edward Baker, Kogan Page, London, forthcoming June 1996

Last, and most certainly least in this exalted company, a practical guide to the lucrative area of theory training. This book does not assume that you have spent years in teaching college or that you want to master *Gestalt* learning; it is about everything from how to use flip charts to dealing with trouble makers in class; and, of course, making lots of money.

APPENDIX 4
USEFUL CONTACTS

Part Four Services

A company devoted entirely to the sales needs of the ADI. Facilities include sales training courses, sales aids, distance learning packs, books, videos, telesales training, insurance, rescue packages and much, much more.

Tel: 0114 250 9217 or 0378 368570

Glen Mcoy, Personal Coaching for ADIs

Personal effectiveness techniques including sales and marketing for the business, time planning and organisation, specialist self-development skills, some of which can be passed on to pupils.

Tel: 01756 799903

Index